THE DEFINITIVE CHIEF FINANCIAL OFFICER

How They can Transform your Business

Mark Gruner

Green Bridge Publishing

FREE GIFT

As a thank you for buying this book we are offering you this free guide to download - insert following address into browser.
Scan QR Code

To my wife.

"There's no question over the last year this new wave of technologies has had an impact on CFO decision making. CFOs are really working to get their arms around all of it and we've seen this not only through our survey but client interactions. If you think about the CFO's role in the last five to 10 years, more and more responsibility has been put on their plate. They need to grasp and understand these new technologies because they are ultimately the chief allocator of capital in these organizations. The CFO is in a position where they have to make choices, and articulate their rationale to the CEO and the board as to how they arrived at their recommendations."

SANDY COCKRELL, GLOBAL LEADER OF THE CFO PROGRAM OF
DELOITTE

CONTENTS

INTRODUCTION

This book will cover the role a CFO plays in an organization. How this critical role works with the CEO and how the CFO can have a significant and positive effect on the whole company. The CFO wears many hats, but one of the most critical roles that they take is ensuring they provide good advice to the CEO. The CFO's relationship with the CEO can be one that can make or break the company. This relationship must be healthy and productive.

Role of CFO

We will demonstrate the role that the CFO plays with regards to financial analysis and ensuring that all managers and unit heads are receiving accurate, timely, and relevant financial reports to ensure the best outcomes for their departments or units. The successful CFO must ensure that the systems exist so that reports can be delivered to the right decision-makers on time. The reports delivered should be relevant and actionable.

This book will be of benefit to anyone who is a CFO or would like to become a CFO. You may be a CFO and the situation you are in is not ideal. Do you have a proper reporting line? Do you have the proper oversight to the board? Are you reporting directly to the CEO? There are a lot of problem areas, that you can look to address even before you sign the contract and accept to be the CFO of the company. It would be much easier to correct at the beginning before any issues start to arise.

Effective Leader

How can you be an effective leader as the CFO? Learn who your most important clients are and learn how to meet their expectations and exceed them. The best way to exceed expectations is to deliver the results that they did not even realize they needed.

Listening - a critical strength

Often, when going into meetings the successful CFO will listen to what his internal clients need in terms of reporting. He will then ask a few questions to get clarity and then meet with his team to discuss. The first thing on his or her agenda is to figure out why do their clients need these reports, what are they trying to achieve. This is sometimes obvious, but where it is not obvious, it may be wise to seek clarity. Once, you understand the reason for their request, the next thing to consider would be whether their requested reports best answers that need. Perhaps there is another report that will suit their needs better. The successful CFO will go beyond just the request and get to the rationale and find the best response. All of their needs must be met, and then some additional needs that they may not have thought about, by achieving this you will surpass expectations. The average CFO just gets the clients what they ask for, while the successful CFO goes far beyond that. They understand the rationale and then deliver far beyond the request.

This book highlights areas where a CFO should be successful. As well, for CEOs, it highlights the best type of working relationships to have between a CEO and CFO and why this partnership is critical for success. It also explains why a direct reporting line from the CFO to the CEO may not always be the most efficient.

Scaling your Business

Anyone who is creating a business and wanting to scale that business further can benefit by understanding how a CFO can help a company and also when it is time to hire a CFO and when it is not the right time to hire. The company must first be able to afford a CFO and must be able to benefit from the costs of having one. The cost-benefit of hiring a CFO must be positive. This book also covers ways to have the benefits of a CFO without the high costs of hiring one, with services such as Remote CFO. This would be ideal for smaller companies that are growing and can afford to incur some expense but not yet in a situation where they can afford a full-time CFO. We also cover ways to get help when in the very early stages of a business.

Finance people often work on specific tasks and may not always be exposed to the big picture that a CFO is exposed to. This is incorrect and the CFO should always present to all their staff the whole picture, even if the staff does not use it in their day-to-day activities. Any finance person that wants to advance their career should understand the concepts in this book and should work towards advancing themselves in every respect. You do not have to be the CFO to be a leader, one can apply these leadership qualities at the manager level and also at the cashier level. By demonstrating that you are helping out the whole team and taking on the greater good of the company and the finance team as a whole, as opposed to only your area of work, you can showcase to the CFO your leadership and this will lead to more responsibilities being given to you, which in turn can lead to a promotion.

PREFACE

It was my first role as CFO for a nonprofit called Commission for Real Property Claims for Displaced Persons and Refugees (CRPC). Up until that point I had held roles as a finance manager or senior auditor roles. This would be a lot more responsibility, was I ready for this challenge? I remember applying for this role, that I felt perfectly suited for, despite it being a big step up from my current role. It was such a large step up that my boss at that time applied for the same role. I purposely did not apply until my boss was turned down. I then applied. I was accepted and started to work a few weeks later.

First Official CFO
Joining CRPC as its first official CFO was slightly intimidating but at the same time, I was fearless and eager to make some progress. When I arrived at my desk on the first day, I asked which accounting software are we using. I was given some spreadsheets in excel. I asked to see the vouchers, there were none. I asked to see our policies and there were none. I asked who prepared the excel spreadsheets and it was a bookkeeper without proper training, although without any training she did a good job, but far below what was needed to manage a complex organization as CRPC.

Everything that I requested either did not exist or was nowhere near the shape it needed to be in, to handle the task at hand. I had a meeting with my team, the full finance team consisted of two people, one who made payments, hence a cashier and the other who did much of the data entry. The data entry person was about 19 years old and not trained properly in accounting but was smart and able to learn what needed to be done. The cashier was a middle-aged woman, who was very kind and a strong bookkeeper but was also not a trained accountant.

I should also mention, that this job was based in Sarajevo, Bosnia and it was around August of 1998, this was a few years after the war in the Balkans which had led to many families fleeing their homes or worse. CRPC was set up as Annex 7 of the Dayton Peace Agreement to decide on property claims for those people that were forced to flee. Bosnia, was a part of the former Yugoslavia which was a former communist country and as such, the concept of accounting was quite different compared with Western standards, hence, roles like a CPA did not really exist yet, not in any formal sense.

The Challenge
This was definitely going to be a major challenge and I was loving it!

I had no mentor to teach me how to prepare these things, I had no predecessor to call on, I had very few staff to be able to support me at that time. I did not have an ERP system let alone an accounting system to record transactions, there were no policies and there was not even an existing payment voucher system. In essence, I was starting with a blank slate, but the company already was in existence for almost two years. I looked at the calendar, it was August, I realized that our audit was less than seven months away and we had nothing to start with. I was an auditor not that long ago and knew what they would need and could see that we had nothing to support our transactions other than a bank statement and these excel spreadsheets that were just a simple recording of expenses.

What was missing?

I made a list of what we were missing and went ahead and started to get everything that we needed. I met with my boss, the CEO, who was very supportive. I said that I will need to hire two or three new staff and would need to create a full set of policies to be approved by yourself and our board. I also needed to purchase an accounting software package. I did not know which one at the time but would figure that out in the coming weeks.

Within a few weeks, I made a few hires. Within a few months, I put in all of the major policies that governed finance and accounting which were unanimously approved. I put in a software package, I chose the least expensive option and it worked out very well. I created vouchers and had my team prepare vouchers for all transactions going forward and as well restate the prior year and a half worth of transactions to the best of their abilities.

We worked all kinds of hours and restated prior vouchers for months, at the same time preparing all the bank reconciliations and cash reconciliations. For any funds that could not be accounted for we kept a running total. By February 1999, we were all caught up, our accounting system worked extremely well. We prepared and approved all prior bank reconciliations and cash reconciliations. The missing cash amounted to about $46. The CEO said that he would gladly fund this missing money and he did. He said something like, I remember one time taking out $50 that the cashier gave me and perhaps it was not recorded, or something to that effect and winked. In the end, I think the two of us were more than pleased that after a year and a half of having no proper systems in place, the only money that we could not account for was $46.

Auditors Visit

The next month the auditors came. I gave them all of their working papers prepared in advance, they had our accounts receivables, our bank statements, our bank reconciliations, our fixed assets, our policies, basically all they could want. After a week of their doing their audit, we took them out to dinner as is customary. The head of the audit team told me, "Mark, this company, I don't recognize it from last year. Last year, the systems were so bad, we struggled to issue an opinion, there was a two-week debate whether we should issue a denial of opinion. You were by far our weakest client, today, you are now one of our best prepared and strongest client. All within some months - congratulations."

All the hard work was a success!

I learned how to be a successful CFO basically by being thrown into the fire and having to learn overnight. The one thing that was a great help was my boss, Steven Segal. He gave me two critical things, he gave me full support and trust as well he gave me the room to do what I needed to do. He had a great attitude and together we made that organization work. Unfortunately, he passed away a number of years ago, but I will never forget the lessons I learned working with him. I will always remember him fondly, he had a great sense of humor and was a great person to work with.

The reason that I am writing this book is to illustrate my journey and how I became a successful CFO. I have had situations that were very successful and also situations that were very challenging and some that were less successful, but at each point, it led me to be a better finance person and CFO. The goal is to pass on this knowledge to the next generation and to learn from some of my successes as well as learn from some of my failures. My first job as a CFO was a great success, a big part of that was having a successful CEO who believed in me and trusted my vision. I have also been in situations where my supervisor or CEO was not the strongest and some were even quite weak. It is important to understand what you can do to resolve these situations before they become too difficult to resolve.

DISCLAIMER

The information provided in this book is for informational and educational purposes only. Nothing in this book can be construed as advice. The authors and owners of this book cannot be construed to make an advisor relationship with any reader.

The material contained in this book is for instructional purposes only. None of the material is, or should be regarded as advice. Accordingly, no person should rely on any of the contents within this book without first obtaining specific advice from the author and publisher, employees and agents accept no responsibility to any person who acts or relies in any way on any of the material without first obtaining specific advice.

The information within this book is provided on an "as is", "as available" basis without warranties of any kind, express or implied, including, but not limited to, those of TITLE, MERCHANTABILITY, FITNESS FOR A PARTICULAR PURPOSE or NON-INFRINGEMENT or any warranty arising from a course of dealing, usage, or trade practice. No oral advice or written information provided shall create a warranty; nor shall readers of this book rely on any such information or advice. This publication is not intended to be a contract, explicit or implied, and the author and publisher reserves the right to make changes in the information contained.

The user assumes all responsibility and risk for the use of the information contained within this book. We accept no liability or responsibility to any person as a consequence of any reliance upon the information contained in this book. Under no circumstances, including negligence, shall anyone involved in creating or maintaining this book and the information contained within be liable for any direct, indirect, incidental, special or consequential damages, or loss profits that result from the use or inability to use the information contained within this book. Nor shall they be liable for any such damages including, but not limited to, reliance by a reader on any information obtained via the book or related website; or that result from mistakes, omissions, interruptions, deletion of files, viruses, errors, defects, or failure of performance, communications failure, theft, destruction or unauthorised access. States or Countries which do not allow some or all of the above limitations of liability, liability shall be limited to the greatest extent allowed by law.

CHAPTER 1 - WHY IS A CFO CRITICAL

"Operating a global business in a fast-changing world, you have to be grounded real-time in the external environment, have complete transparency, be fact-based and working with a great, collaborative team."

- BOB SHANKS, THE CFO OF FORD

The CFO plays a crucial role in every company even those that do not have an official role of CFO. In this case, someone is acting as the CFO. It could be the owner who is acting as both the CEO and CFO with smaller companies. Some CEOs act also as CFO, hence, even when you do not have one, you have a person who is providing the services of a CFO.

The main function of a CFO is to lead the overall financial function of the company. This entails being in charge of the past and present financial situation and has a key role in determining the future financial situation.

Reports

The CFO ensures that the financial reports are correct and delivered promptly. This ensures that the CEO can make decisions as to how to best manage the company.

The CFO prepares cost-benefit analyses to ensure that investment outlays of a company are done so, wisely. The CFO will use net present value analysis to see whether an investment today will yield good results tomorrow. This is a critical function of the CFO. This is the best way to understand whether a decision made today is wise. Many objective factors play into the cost-benefit analysis and also many subjective factors, both must be weighed appropriately.

Forecasting

Forecasting is a necessary tool that a CFO must deliver on. It is not only important to know where we were yesterday and where we are today, but also to estimate where we will be tomorrow. Without this, both the CFO and CEO will not be able to make informed decisions and will not be able to know whether past decisions are valid or not until it is too late to make any necessary adjustments.

For publicly held companies, the CFO ensures compliance with all requirements from the stock exchange, shareholder requirements, tax reporting requirements, and many others. This is a critical function to ensure that the company is in good standing and can signal if the company is facing problems or is doing better than expected. These will have a significant effect on the stock price.

The CFO provides leadership and direction to the finance team. The CFO ensures that the team has a clear vision of where they should be going and ensures that they are on the correct path. The CFO should provide the correct motivation to team members to ensure tasks are properly achieved. It is also important to be able to assess talent and to assess those that are poorly delivering. The talented financial staff can be rewarded with further responsibilities and potentially a promotion. With poorly performing staff it is important to get to the reason for the lack of performance. It could be that the staff member lacks training or is not motivated or it could be that they are not a good fit for their role. Then the CFO can determine which is the best method to improve the situation, it may be a simple matter of getting the necessary training for the staff member or it may mean helping the staff member realize that this role is not a great fit. It could be the case that the staff member is lacking appropriate training, which could be resolved quickly.

Critical Role for Company

The CFO is critical to the company as the company needs to be profitable, in the long run, to be able to sustain itself and present a going concern. A company does not have to be profitable today nor does it have to be profitable tomorrow, but a company does need to see a vision in the future where it is profitable. If a company cannot present the future profitability within a few years, it will have a very difficult time attracting investors and getting potential shareholders to purchase its stock. This is a critical function of the CFO. If there is no likely outcome where the company is earning profits then that company will have difficulty in getting funding or selling its stock. The investors will have a hard time keeping the company afloat and once the funds run out, the company will end up going bankrupt. It is always a bad sign when your assets less liabilities or your equity has more value than the value of your future earnings. This is a sure sign that it is better to close down and sell the assets for a profit. This means that your equity is greater than the expected future earnings, a very bad sign. In essence, it means that by selling your assets and covering your liabilities or closing down, you will earn more than running the company. Whenever this occurs, it is a sure sign that the company will soon close its doors.

Demonstrating Future Value

The CFO must be able to show the future value of a company. They must look at the financial situation of the company over the past few years, look at it today, and then project where they will be a few years down the road. The CFO of a company may forecast that there will be losses for the next few years, but then there will be significant growth and they will start to have growth and profits after that. The key here is that the projections must look reasonable and then these projections must be met. This is where stock prices can change for the better or worse. If a CFO projects that the deficit this year will be $50 M, next year it will be $20 M, then $10 M, then they will be break-even and then they will start profiting $50 M and with a growth in profits at 25% per year for the next ten years. If these numbers are reasonable, then the company could have quite a good valuation. There will be additional risk put on profits far into the future as the estimates into the distant future are far riskier than estimates closer to today. This makes sense as there are far more potential variable in three years time than there are over the next six months.

A company that develops a new app could have many expenses in the first few years and very little revenue, but once the app has been created and then sold, then revenues can start coming in. Hence, it is not unusual for companies to have a couple of years of projected losses before projections start to show profits. The key here is that these projections must be reasonable and based on estimates that are based on concrete facts. As time passes the potential investors will be able to see if the targets are being met or are not being met. Hence, it is critical that the CFO can present a solid picture of the next few years and that they can demonstrate that those targets are being met. It is far better to exceed these targets than to miss the targets. Targets that are exceeded will result in stock price increases while missed targets will give rise to lowered stock prices.

Investments in Capital Assets

The CFO is instrumental in ensuring that capital investments of the company are good for the bottom line, for the long term. They will achieve this by performing a net present value or a cost-benefit analysis. Hence, if the company is deciding whether to expand its operations in another country or add a new business line. The CFO must determine financially if this makes sense. The end decision will lie with the CEO but the critical analysis will be done by the CFO and their teams. It will be important to estimate the overall costs necessary to implement and the future revenues that are likely to be derived by this endeavor. If the net present value of revenues exceeds the net present value of costs to be incurred, then the investment is likely to provide overall benefit. As well, other, subjective factors are necessary to take into account, such as reputation risk. A gain in market share should be factored into the overall increase in revenues. There are times when a future benefit is hard to estimate or measure, in this case, a range of possible values should be used. When there is no way to gauge a reasonable estimate of the benefit, then it should be simply stated as a subjective benefit and not quantified. When the quantitative analysis is very close, then the qualitative analysis may be used to sway the decision one way or another.

The CFO must have a strong understanding of accounting and auditing techniques since they will be primarily responsible for dealing with external audits and auditors. It is much easier to accomplish this if you can converse fluently in the language of auditing. By knowing which areas of your financial interpretations are on solid ground and those on less solid ground, this will give you a strong base to ensure that you can justify those areas that are stronger and those areas that are more on shaky ground to let go. If the auditors feel that you are arguing with every single issue, they will likely do the same with you and your audit will not go as smoothly as anticipated. The audited report is very critical to ensure a strong reporting history and to ensure the narrative that you are setting is correct. It is critical that the audit not require significant changes within the financial statements that may cause a potential investor to think twice.

Financial Integrity

The CFO is critical to any company as they are ensuring the financial integrity of the company. They are ensuring that financial reporting is accurate, understandable, and delivered on time. This is critical for the CEO to be able to make the best decision possible, they can only achieve this when the CFO achieves their roles. This is also critical, so that when poor decisions are made, they can be corrected before too much damage is incurred.

By ensuring the best investment decisions are being made the CFO is worth his or her weight in gold. If there is a person to be able to say that this investment is good and that investment poses problems, then that person would be the CFO. This alone can save the company significant sums and months of work for the company. For this to work well, the CEO must understand and pay heed to the CFO and their recommendations. In unusual cases, where there may be an underlying qualitative reason that the investment should be made, then perhaps there could be a disagreement, but in most cases, the CEO should agree with the CFO, unless the CEO feels that process was undertaken incorrectly. This should be extremely rare in a well-functioning company. There is also a case where the CEO may have a gut feeling about something, and may decide to do something else. This is fine but should be well-documented, as these gut feelings can end up being quite costly.

Success of Company

The overall success of a company is very much linked with the overall financial success of that company. A financially successful company is often viewed as being successful overall, and vice versa. It is clear that the financial functions of the company fall under the responsibility of the CFO, but the overall success of the company falls under the CEO. Generally speaking, the CFO reports to the CEO but sometimes they report solely to the board, or they may report both to the CEO and the board. This is where there could be some level of conflict. If both have different views on the way that the company will be profitable. Due to this relationship and these understandings, the CFO and CEO must work well together or there is a strong board that assists in this process. It would be rather difficult to imagine a company working well, where the CFO and CEO are not working well together and vice-versa.

Different Point of View

The challenge here is that should both the CEO and CFO have a different vision of the financial future of the company, while the CFO generally reports to the CEO, one may feel that the CFO should agree with the CEO. The other view is that the CEO should not micro-manage his teams and hence should agree with the CFO. There is no right answer here. In reality, sometimes the CFO is correct and sometimes the CEO is correct. Ultimately though, when the CEO decides to ignore the input given from the CFO, then that CEO should be very sure that he or she is correct. It is one thing to be wrong, but it is another thing to be presented with the right answer and then choosing the wrong answer. This should only be used when the CEO is almost certain that the CFO is wrong. Ideally, they would be able to explain their case and both would agree.

In my experience, working with strong CEOs they usually agreed with me, while working with weaker CEOs they are the ones that were more likely to disagree and more likely to be wrong, as well.

Less Talented CEO

It is an interesting dynamic that the weaker CEO tended to be less self-confident, in other words, they also could see that they were weak, but this would make them more likely to try to prove their worth by making their own decisions. It almost never worked out for the weaker CEOs. They were more likely to go their own way and not pay heed to advice from the CFO and they were also more likely to make poor choices. Being a poor CEO, caused them to have insecurity issues, which caused them to try to prove themselves more. A good recipe for poor results. I never witnessed this situation ending well.

CHAPTER 2 - ELEMENTS OF A CFO

"Early to bed and early to rise make a man healthy, wealthy, and wise."

- BENJAMIN FRANKLIN

A successful CFO must have many strengths. Some are skills that we can classify as soft skills and other as hard skills. The strong CFO must have a strong business sense and know when a decision is good and when a decision is poor. They must fully understand all the concepts in accounting, auditing, valuations, and management. It is key that this individual can communicate well within his department, with other departments, and both internally and externally.

Team Building

Being capable of recognizing talent and also recognizing weaknesses is critical to being able to motivate any team. The successful CFO must have exemplary leadership skills. They must be able to have a vision and then articulate that vision and inspire others to take on that vision. If the CFO is capable of having a vision but not capable of inspiring others to take on that vision, the CFO will not be a great leader. As well, if the CFO is capable to inspire others to take on a vision but is not capable of creating a proper and valid vision, then they will also not make a great leader. By being a great leader, the strong CFO will be able to implement their vision and have it become successful. In other words, you need to be able to come up with the right vision and also be able to inspire others to take up your vision.

Inspiring Others

Inspiring others to follow their vision must work in three directions, it must work from the CFO down to their teams, it must work across all departments and it must work up to the supervisor of the CFO, hence, both the CEO and the Board must agree with this vision. Once, this vision is accepted then it is just a matter of implementation of the vision. This is where good management skills come in. The strong CFO must be a strong leader and a great manager. The teams must be motivated and must fully understand the roles that they play to achieve this vision.

Business Acumen

The strong CFO must have a thorough understanding of business with a focus on the business that they are in. The strong understanding of business is the critical one of the two here. The person must understand how to get more market share and how to invest wisely to get more revenues and profits. It is not sufficient that a CFO just lets things run along, the strong CFO must always be pushing for more and pushing for more profits.

A CFO must be able to convince the CEO that their vision is correct. It would be impossible to have a strong CFO without a strong connection with the CEO. A strong CEO should be one that can motivate his teams and probably the most important person on his team is the CFO. A good working relationship is a must and for that to work, the CEO mustn't micromanage the CFO. This way the relationship can blossom and the team can go on to accomplish great things. This would improve market share and improve profitability.

Know the Numbers

The strong CFO must know his numbers better than anyone. He must understand what works financially in the company, what is struggling, and what simply does not work and will not work. This way they can cut out what is not working and use those resources to put towards what is working and what is struggling. If resources are spent on business segments that will not work, this will be a waste of time and resources. The CFO must be able to tell a team that their side of the business is not working and if things are not fixed within a few weeks we will be closing this segment and focusing our efforts elsewhere. Proper resource allocation is critical for the success of a company. If a company cannot figure out which aspects of their business are working and which are not, then that company will not get too far.

Knowing how to improve certain business lines is also a key for a successful CFO. For example, if you have a business line of selling cell phones, but it is not yet profitable, one needs to be able to look at the reasons for the lack of success. Is it the product itself, is it the costs of manufacturing, or is it advertising. The CFO should provide resources to get to the root of the problem. If the problem is that the phone cannot be manufactured at a price that would make it competitive for a certain niche, then there is little that can be done. You could spend money on advertising and even get to the point where that product is profitable, however, starting with a product that is not competitive is not a wise jumping-off point. It would be far better to invest if the product is far superior to most smartphones in that price range. If you are selling in the under $200 range, you do not need to beat smartphones that are selling in ranges of $800 - $1,000, but you should be beating all phones selling under $100 and most, if not all, phones selling under $200, in order to be competitive.

If you do have a competitive phone selling under $200 but it is not widely known, it is important to understand what will be the costs to get that phone more widely known and the effects on sales. One should also think about the long-run, if you spend $ 10 M to get an increase in market share but do not recover your investment on this phone, can those customers buy into your next phone. It is not simply a question of will I get more sales that will cover my advertising costs. One must think about the costs of attaining a new customer versus the cost of retaining a customer.

Understanding of Business
Understanding every major element of the business is critical for a strong CFO. They should be well versed in all aspects, from manufacturing to sales to delivery. At each point along the process, there is room for improvement. Often the small tweaks can lead to major results and can be the difference from a profitable product or service to one that is not profitable. Are there areas in manufacturing that are wasteful or can be improved upon? Is advertising effective and efficient? Can these be improved upon? What is the cost of acquiring a customer? What is the lifetime value of a customer?

Reporting and analysis are key strengths of a strong CFO, the CFO would not need to do these functions themself, except in smaller entities. The CFO would need to oversee teams that provide this function, but the CFO would need to ensure that it is done correctly and accurately. The CFO and CEO must have strong financial analysis to be able to make informed decisions to run the business correctly. This is a key factor, a strong CFO must understand these computations and look at how they are performed to ensure that they make sense. If there are areas that do not correlate with the analysis given, the CFO must be able to get his teams to dive in further to justify the numbers or show where some further analysis is needed.

Critically speaking, perhaps the two most important aspects of a CFO are his abilities in business and his ability to look at the analysis and make an informed decision. His business savvy will also help with the analysis and alert them to times where further analysis may be required. Analytical skills are tantamount, just as business skills are. The skills of persuasion and leadership are also critical but if you cannot understand the right answer then whether you can lead or not is a secondary issue. The strongest CFOs are strong in every element, but being able to determine the proper solution is probably the most important strength of all. Without this strength, it would be hard for any CFO to be successful.

CHAPTER 3 - TEAM BUILDING

"From a finance hiring perspective, you need to hire the best athletes who want to be part of a high-performance team. You also need leaders who are superhuman. We accomplish things every day that have never been done. Roles change constantly, so you need team members who are flexible, thrive in a world of explosive growth and are simply hungry to learn and grow their careers."

— BRIAN ROBERTS, CFO OF LYFT

Another critical skill of a successful CFO is the ability to create strong teams and partnerships. Alongside leadership, the CFO must know how to build successful teams that they can rely on. The most important team for the CFO would be their Finance team. They must be able to rely on their finance team to fulfill all the finance functions at the highest level and there must be a number of staff that can take the role of CFO while they are away from the office. They could be away on a business trip or on vacation. It is critical that the CFO has trained their teams well and that they can rely both on their abilities and that they will act in good faith.

Building a Strong Finance Team

If a CFO cannot build a strong finance team that they can rely on, this will be a sure sign that the CFO will be a failure. The CFO must be given all the tools necessary to achieve this. If a staff member is not qualified or not pulling their weight, the CFO must be allowed to move them out or to find a way to motivate them. If these tools are not provided to the CFO then it will be that much more difficult to build a strong team.

If there is a very negative person on the team, for whatever reason, perhaps the person was passed over for promotion, the CFO should try to correct this attitude, but there are times when there is no available ways to correct the situation other than moving the person out. The CFO should have the power to do so and to find a replacement that they feel can do the job best. It is important to ensure that the team is properly motivated. Some staff may feel loyal to the predecessor or may feel they should have been given a chance, but if they cannot recover from this poor attitude, the CFO needs to ship them out. The next step is putting the right staff in the right places. If you have a staff member that cannot perform their role but could perform another role better, the best time to make this shift would be immediately. It is very possible that right at the start of a new CFO taking over there will be some shifting around in the finance team and even some rumbling and some people being asked to leave. This should be done during the first few months and then the time would be to work on getting this new team up and running. It is critical that there is a mutual respect between you and the team. You must protect every team member and every team member must protect you. It is important that the team understands that a team is successful when everyone is successful. There is no maverick on this team, all are stars.

Developing Strong Partnerships

With a strong team in place, then the CFO can also make sure to develop strong partnerships. The first one would be with the CEO, this is the most critical partnership. The CFO should keep the CEO abreast of all challenges and successes that the CFO is dealing with. The CFO should understand at what level is the CEO interested, most CEOs prefer a very brief high level overview and that is what you should start with. If the CEO has a desire for more information, then it is fine to give them that information. Ideally the CEO would just want to see the picture at 30,000 feet. It is not great for you or for the CEO to start getting into any detailed discussion. This may prove counterproductive. You need to just say that all is under control, just giving you an update. However, the moment something is not in control or may lead to something not in control, then you should expect to discuss further.

Major Partners
Other key partners will be the Chief Operations Officer (COO), the Chief Information Officer (CIO) and the Director of Human Resources, along with the CEO these will form your major internal partnerships and it would be critical to have regular updates with all positions. The COO may be the one that you are dealing with the most as many of the things that you would like to accomplish will require input from this role. If you are planning on updating the rolling stock, the COO will be a critical partner in this process. If there is a plan to overhaul the production facility, the COO will also play a critical role. It is ideal for these two roles to have a meeting every Monday to find out what is on the agenda for the week and also for the next few upcoming months. The partnership with the COO would likely be the second most critical partner within the company and definitely a critical partner in any company.

The CIO partnership is also a critical one. The CFO must be able to find ways that they can improve their reporting and the best way is to create a strong partnership with the CIO. Any change to the ERP or financial reporting system of a company will require some assistance with the CIO. Knowing that they are in your corner and will take the extra steps for you will be that much more of an advantage. The CIO and their teams would be also an excellent source of brainstorming to see how the reporting and ERP systems can be enhanced. The partnering with the CIO is another crucial partnership for the success of the CFO role and success of the company, as a whole.

Working with Human Resources

In order for the CFO to be able to achieve all the necessary movements within the team by either removing staff that are not performing or have a negative attitude and bringing in the right staff, the CFO must create a strong partnership with the Director of HR or the Chief Human Resource Officer (CHRO), in order to implement these changes easier. This partnership is critical, the CHRO must see that you are doing these changes for the better of the company. This can help if you have already discussed your plans with this partner. If the CFO has not built strong relations with the CHRO and the CHRO feels that you should put more time to that relationship, it may be that the CHRO will take a stand against your actions and this will cause you additional time and efforts. It is best to avoid these types of conflicts and build strong relationships and partnerships right from the start. Your ability to get your team right will require strong partnerships with the CHRO. This is a critical partnership in any company.

With the right partnerships you will be able build your successful team. Then you will be in the position of being able to deliver that much better for each partner, for your team, for the CEO, and for the company, overall. These are critical steps to achieve success as a CFO.

CHAPTER 4 - CFO MINDSET

"Finance, conceptually, really sits outside of the organization. What I mean by that is we have to be Switzerland, a little bit—we're supposed to be the objective person."

— SUE VESTRI, CFO OF GREENPHIRE

It is important that the mindset of a CFO be very optimistic. The person should be optimistic and realistic but not naive. The CFO should always be looking for ways to make things better they should never settle for the status quo. If a CFO believes that things cannot get any better than they are today then it is time for that CFO to retire. If you do not believe that things can get better then things definitely will not get better.

Optimist and Realistic

It does not mean that the CFO should be optimistic to the point of being oblivious or unrealistic. If it is clear that things are now working well. The CFO must recognize that, but also must be able to see ways that the situation can be improved upon. In very poor situations, there is always a possible decision to scrap the business and start over. This would be the case where things are unworkable or where a segment is becoming unprofitable. This does not mean that the CFO is not an optimist the CFO is being optimistic in saying that if we divert our resources over here then we can do better.

One must be able to see the areas that work, and the areas that do not work, and aim to make those areas that are working, work even better. The areas that do not work should start to work and the areas that are never going to work should be closed down immediately. This will ensure that the company is using its resources to the best extent possible.

Comparing Results

When we look at a company that is successful and is driving a lot of profit compared to its equity then it is most likely due to the company working extremely well. If we compare two companies that are both selling smartphones, if both companies have $20 M of equity and the first company is about to drive $5 M in profits while the second is only able to drive $2 M in profits, then we would be able to conclude that the first company is more effective than the second. At least for today, but the reality is you would need to see the projections over the next five years to be able to gauge. The second company may be focusing on gaining market share to get more profits down the road and may be projecting to have profits of $10 M in three years. For simplicity, if we assume that all future years will have the same profits as today, in this scenario, it is clear that the first company is doing better than the second company.

Debt to Equity Ratio

We cannot only look at equity to get a good estimate of how well a company is doing. If we look at the debt to equity ratio of these two companies we may see another issue altogether. If we assume that the first company has $100 M in assets, hence, $80 M in liabilities and $20 M in equity, while the second company has $20 M in assets, and no liabilities, and hence, $20 M in equity. The first company is profiting $5 M with $100 M in assets, while the second company is generating $2 M with $20 M in assets. This now becomes a bit more complex when we estimate which company is doing better. What if the second company was able to take out debt and maintain the same profit per its assets. Hence, to drive $5 M in profits it would need to have $50 M in assets. Then the balance sheet would have $50 M in assets, $30 M in liabilities, and $ 20 M in equity. Now, despite that they are profiting the same amount per year, it is the second company that is doing better by having a lower debt to equity ratio yet delivering the same results.

Being able to generate more profits while keeping risk to a minimum is a key function of the successful CFO.

Risks

When a company is performing very well by most standards the company likely has both a successful CFO and a successful CEO who work well together. It is almost impossible to imagine a company functioning well where either the CEO or the CFO is not performing well. By the same token when a company is underperforming, likely, either or both the CEO and CFO are not performing as they should. There are cases where the company has suffered due to circumstances beyond their control, this would be the one exception to the general rule, but most failures of a company are due to events that are within their control. If we look at a famous example, Blockbuster became bankrupt, but before going bankrupt it was offered to purchase Netflix at a bargain price. Both the CFO and CEO could not see where the future was and let this opportunity pass by. It is estimated that the price of Netflix was offered to Blockbuster for $ 50 M. Today, that price would be a steal. Being able to peek into the future and see what risks you face is a key component of good financial management. This would be an example of where both the CFO and CEO were probably competent by most definitions but failed miserably. In the end, when you have such advantages and fail miserably, the overall grade can only be assessed as a major failure. Ironically, BlockBuster was offered the opportunity to purchase the company that put them out of business and they did not buy it.

Finding Opportunities
Being able to look for opportunities is a key strength that all good CFOs and CEOs must-have. One must be looking out for future risks but also future opportunities. Blockbuster probably felt that they were doing everything right and that it could not get any better. This feeling is exactly the time when you will get hit with something that may not have been in your sight. In the case of Blockbuster and Netflix, the threat was in their sight and they could have purchased it for an almost give-away price.

Hindsight is always 20/20, but when looking at the facts that were available at the time, it was clear that internet connections were getting much stronger and that at some point very soon it would be very practical to be able to stream movies from the internet. Having a paid service for this would mean that people could choose their movies from their living room without having to get into their car and choose a movie. It also meant that if you chose a movie you did not like, you could simply choose another movie. There was no need to return movies. This was a clear blunder and a very costly one for all the shareholders of Blockbuster.

CHAPTER 5 - PREREQUISITES TO EXCELLENCE

For the CFO to succeed they will need certain prerequisites. When the CFO first starts at a new company they must have strong finance teams that can be relied upon. There must be a strong reporting system that is both accurate and timely. The reporting should be able to have an estimate of the major key performance indicators (KPI) for the company and the finance teams. If these do not exist, then the CFO must ensure that they put these in place as the first order of business.

Required Support

The CFO must have strong support from both the CEO and the Board. It will be a challenge for the CFO to be effective without this proper support. The CEO must also be strong, if the CEO is not strong in both ability and character, then it will be a challenge for the CFO to succeed. When faced with a weak CEO the CFO has only three options, the first is to try to completely influence the decisions of the CEO in most aspect, the second option is that they can advocate for a change in the CEO, not an easy goal to accomplish. The third option available to the CFO is to leave. This may be the best and only real option for a CFO who is put to work with a weak

CEO. If the Board does not also see that the CEO is weak and the company is failing, then the best option is to leave.

Business Proposition of Company

The company must be capable of success and not too far down the wrong road. If a company is incurring significant losses, has a large amount of debt, it will be very hard to turn this around especially if they are very near or already defaulting on their loans. The CFO may be able to turn things around, but sometimes it may be too little too late. A good doctor may be able to cure a very sick patient, but there is a time where it may be too late for a doctor to save a patient if medical help is not sought on time.

Having the best CFO in the world will not assist much if there are not certain prerequisites for success. Success likelihood will be increased greatly by having the best CFO, but if all the prerequisites are missing, that success will be very unlikely. It would be comparable to the best Chess player in the world playing a very talented but average player. The World Champion of Chess would have a very high chance of beating an average good player in a regular chess game. However, if the World Champion of Chess was playing without a Queen, without any Bishops or Knights, his or her chance of success would drop to almost zero. He would be capable of beating someone that never played before but even a relatively average player who has played the game more than 50 times would be able to beat him. To illustrate this point, if the Grand Master in Chess, who has a rating above 2,500 were to play a strong player let us say a rating of 1,800 and he was told to play White but he was missing those pieces. His first and only move would be to resign immediately. Whenever a player is down so many significant pieces, unless there is a clear set of moves to victory, the only option is to quit. In chess, quitting is seen as a respectable thing to do, it is telling your opponent that I respect your ability and I will not extend the known outcome. It is very different from a sport like tennis, where even if you are far behind, you can still win, or any sport for that matter. With chess, it is very different, if you are far behind, generally you cannot win, unless your opponent makes a major mistake, which is extremely unlikely or there are a set of forced moves that will allow for mate, which generally is unlikely.

Cannot Solve all Issues

In other words, just having the best CFO in the world would not be enough if there are not prerequisites there for success. The strong CFO would, after some time, recognize that the prerequisites are not there and then leave. One of the key requirements would be having a strong CEO who knows how to run the business. If this requirement is not there, then it would be like playing chess without the Queen or even without the King. If the finance team is not that strong, this one can be corrected but it will take time. The CFO can rebuild the team but at the beginning, it will cause the CFO to work with one hand tied behind his back. The CFO will not be able to operate at full efficiency. Having weakness in your finance teams is the better problem to have, as you can directly resolve that issue over time. A strong CFO can turn weak finance teams to strong finance teams within a year if need be. The CFO cannot change a weak CEO to a strong CEO within a year or even within years, especially if the weak CEO is not open to criticism or hearing alternative ways forward. Which is usually the first reason for a weak CEO. The effect of a strong CEO and weak CEO can be easily seen by looking at Apple, Steve Jobs had a significant impact on that company and turned it around while it was struggling. Choosing the right CEO can greatly affect your company and also choosing the wrong CEO can be a disaster for your company.

The business proposition of the company may be wrong and it may be that the whole concept needs changing quickly to become profitable. The company may now be in a business that is obsolete or has never been able to find success. Hence, if the company has been losing money for many years and has not been able to make a break-through, it is important to understand why. Perhaps what they are trying to sell, just is not worth the cost of production. The CFO must review the business model and if the business model just does not work, then it is best to either try to transfer to another model or move into another segment. This is an area that could be a challenge for a CFO but it would not be a nail in the coffin, they would be able to work their way out of this problem and have the company turn-around, but it would require time and resources.

Comparing Efficiency

When comparing the efficiency of two CFOs, it would be important to ensure that they are both on the same level playing field. The CFO who has the ideal situation, a strong CEO, a strong team, and a company that is performing strongly would have a completely unfair advantage compared to a CFO with a weak CEO, a struggling finance team, and a poorly performing company. The weak CEO and poorly performing companies are a dire situation and one that even the best CFO in the world would have trouble fixing. It would not be impossible, however, if you have a CEO that is completely dense and cannot understand the reason, then this is extremely difficult to fix. It would be similar to playing chess but having a person that is on your team but can remove one of your pieces whenever they want to. It is simply an untenable situation.

Capable Board

A Board that is strong and understands the business is also a key prerequisite. They will be able to understand the situation where things are not going properly. They would also be in a position to override and potentially even remove a CEO that is not performing well. This would be your only remedy to a situation of having a very weak CEO. If the Board is not capable of doing their job and removing a weak CEO, then the strong CFO is only left with one option and that would be to leave. The company will likely fail within a few years after the strong CFO has left. Any other strong CFO will face the same challenges and it will only be a weak CFO that would feel comfortable in that environment. The whole executive team will likely face the same issue and all the strong executives will leave. This is one of the reasons a strong CEO is critical to success. He or she sets the tone, if they are weak, then it is a sign for strong executives to leave and weak executives to join or to stay put. This is exactly the wrong message that you want to be setting for the executives. This, in turn, will affect the managers, as the strong managers will not appreciate reporting to weak executives. Sooner than later, the strong managers will begin to leave only to be replaced with weaker managers. The only way to resolve this situation is by replacing the CEO and finding a strong one. The CEO sets the tone for the whole company. The Board is responsible for ensuring that the proper CEO is chosen or acts swiftly to correct a CEO that is not meeting certain standards.

If the CFO can influence the weak CEO, then this is one situation that can be workable. The problem is that often the weak CEO only listens to themselves and this is why they are weak in the first place. If however, the weak CEO does decide that they will listen to the CFO, then this is a workable situation. The CFO can effectively tell the CEO the decisions that need to be made and the CEO will execute them. This can lead to a situation where the CEO is more the figurehead and the CFO is running the company. While this situation may not be ideal, it is a far better situation than the weak CEO not heeding the advice of the strong CFO. In this case, the CFO can become a strong crutch for the weak CEO and the company can thrive. The CEO must be willing to use that crutch. It would also be important that the CFO and CEO are completely confidential with this arrangement. It may be just that the CEO primarily agrees with the CFO or it may be that the CEO asks the CFO in private what he should do. This is a winning situation for the company, for the CFO and the CEO. It may not be the ideal situation but it is a winning situation.

Hence, there is one situation where the strong CFO can work in an environment with a weak CEO and a weak Board, but only in the situation where the CEO primarily defers all decision making to the CFO. Ultimately this is a wise choice for the weak CEO, as they will get the credit for a strong performing company. The CEO will be the final one to make the decisions and hence rightfully get credit. The CFO will feel motivated in this situation as they are having a direct and positive effect on the business. It will also send the correct message to the executive team that they need to be strong and effective. The morale of the company will be improved and there will be a correct message going to staff to become more effective.

This situation will create a positive environment and this will benefit all levels of the company from the executive team to the assistants' team. This will ensure the best possible results and give the company the best chance of success.

Some of the Prerequisites are a Must
The strong CFO will not need all the prerequisites to be successful, but they will need some of the prerequisites to be successful or alternatively a long time to build up the prerequisites on their own. The more of the prerequisites they have the better chance of success, but given a certain level of support and especially coming from the CEO or the Board, then the CFO will be able to create a successful environment over some time. This will then lead the company to success.

CHAPTER 6 – RELATIONSHIP BETWEEN THE CEO AND CFO

Without a doubt, the most important relationship to nourish, for the CFO is their relationship with the CEO. Much of the success or lack of success can be attributed to strong or weak relations with the CEO. The CEO must be able to fully trust and respect the CFO and vice versa. If the CEO does not feel that the CFO respects them, it is very unlikely that they will give respect where none is granted. Hence, much work should be done to ensure a strong relationship is built. It is critical that the CEO knows and understands that the CFO is looking out for them and the company.

Second in Command

When the CEO leaves for a vacation or on a work trip, the CFO should be the first one that the CEO asks to fill in for them. If this is not the case, there could be an issue with the relationship between the two. This should be addressed more quickly than allowing it to fester and become worse. If you are not receiving the necessary support from the CEO, the CFO needs to address this right away. If this is the case, then the CFO should request a meeting with the CEO and ask why does there seem to be some issues that would cause you to feel that either the trust or respect levels are falling. One could ask if there was something that they had done or something that they did not do but should have done. It is often just a misunderstanding that can be cleared up quickly. It may be that the CEO had to leave at the last minute and another executive was in the office and he simply asked them to cover for the CEO. This is a reasonable response but it should be made clear that this may send the wrong message if this is to be repeated. If every time the CEO leaves another executive is put in charge, it may send the message that the CFO is not the second most important member on the team. This will hurt the effectiveness of the CFO.

Support Indicators

This is one indication where the support is not as strong as it should be, but another greater indication would be the number of times that your advice or recommendations are being second-guessed. One must also look at the type of recommendation that is being reviewed more critically. If the correct proposal is the one you recommended and there is still a question whether this is acceptable, then this is another very strong indication of a problem with the relationship. If the answer is completely obvious to you but not to the CEO, then this could be an indication that there are some serious issues. You must address this as swiftly as possible. Whenever the situation is very extreme where the answer is very trivial and both answers would be fine if the CEO is still choosing the other option than the one you recommended when both are equally fine options, then this may also be a sign of the CEO wanting to show that he is the boss, which is somewhat acceptable, but if it is a sign that he does not trust you, then this is not acceptable. You need to keep a mental note of these types of situations and see if there is a pattern. At the end of the day, if the CEO does not have faith in the CFO, it does not matter if the CFO is the most capable in the world, his work will be negatively affected by this weak relationship.

Recognizing a Problem

Once the CFO recognizes that there is a potential problem with the working relationship with the CEO, the CFO must request a meeting with the CEO, to have a frank and difficult conversation. It may be easier to avoid this difficult conversation, but very little good comes from avoiding or delaying any difficult conversations. These are the conversations that one should attend to immediately. It is often the case that there is miscommunication from both sides that can be addressed by discussing the issues right away.

One must try to put themselves into the position of the other. When the CFO feels that they are not getting the trust or respect that they feel they deserve from the CEO, they must put themselves in the position of the CEO and ask whether the problem was something that they inadvertently caused during the past little while. Perhaps there was a small comment that the CEO misunderstood that is the cause of this situation. A lot of times these issues are caused by simple misunderstandings. It may be that the CEO felt that the CFO was disrespectful to the CEO and this is their way of returning the favor. It can be something so banal that it was not even noticed by the CFO. The CEO is a person too, and sometimes they are put in a position with a lot of pressure. Sometimes they are ready for this role and sometimes they are not quite ready. In either case, the CFO should understand this and try to help the CEO, even if the CEO is wrong and coming to the wrong conclusion. It is still important for the CFO to repair the situation and try to move on and develop the best relationship possible.

Critical Relationship

This is often much easier said than it is to accomplish, however, despite any differences you may have, this relationship must be working at full capacity or close to that. If not, the whole success of the CFO will be in jeopardy. If the relationship sours, there will be a tipping point where it will be next to impossible to recover from or it will take too much energy from both sides. The minute that the relationship starts to go south, this will be devastating and next to impossible for the CFO to succeed. If the CFO does have some success in one area, the CEO will not praise the CFO and will look at these results with skepticism or credit the finance team below the CFO and not the CFO. They could say something like, "Your team did a great job." or "Lucky, that you have such a great team.", thus giving all credit to the team and not you. Despite that, you are responsible for your team's success or failure. Then should there be an issue that does not work ideally or fails, the failure will be all put on you. The CEO could say something like, "I thought you would take care of this." or "If you had lead year team better this would not have occurred. Once, these sort of situations start to occur, it may be too late. It is clear that the CEO now has it in for the CFO. It would be good to have a very difficult conversation with the CEO and ask what is the cause of this treatment. The weaker the CEO the more likely is this type of situation.

Equally important is that when the relationship is good between the CFO and the CEO, both work at maintaining a strong relationship. It may be good today but small changes could occur that slowly take a toll on the relationship. The CEO must know that the CFO is there to defend the CEO and can fully trust the CFO. This strong relationship is not only critical to the success of the CFO but it is also critical to the success of the CEO. Hence, if their relationship suffers so too does the company suffer and both the effectiveness of the CEO and CFO suffer. This would be a bad situation all around. Hence, it would be in both of their best interest to address any relationship, trust, or respect issues right away. Once, the two have developed a strong relationship then both can create a strong company and if they are not successful, then it would be the fault of both of them and not the fault of one alone. Ideally, the company would be successful and then both can take part in the credit for this success, while at the same time if the company suffers a setback, both would be partially responsible and there would be no finger-pointing by either the CEO or CFO. It is for this reason, that they must have a good relationship. In this situation, the supervisor is in the driver's seat and hence would have more influence on having a positive relationship or a negative relationship with the CFO. While it may not be the full responsibility of the CEO for a poor relationship it would be the majority of the responsibility since the CEO is the supervisor. If one of your staff and you have a poor relationship, it is quite easy for you to call a meeting with the staff and iron out any issues you may have and then move on to be on better terms. It is far harder, but not impossible, for the person who is reporting to the other person to take an active role in this matter. This is another area where the competence or lack thereof, especially for the CEO, plays a major role in whether the two have a strong relationship or not.

CEO Advisor

The CFO should advise the CEO for any major issues that would affect the productivity, efficiency, or profitability of the company. The CEO must understand the information that he is receiving from the CFO and acts in line with the recommendations given by the CFO. The CEO must be able to trust the data coming from the CFO, that it is accurate and that the conclusions are correct. This is where both trust and respect plays a strong role. It would be quite unusual for the CEO to disregard the analysis of the CFO, but if this is done, the CEO should understand that they are taking a big risk, it is likely that the CFO is correct and by not heeding the recommendations from the CFO, the CEO is taking a very large risk. If the CEO is absolutely certain that they are correct, they should be able to convince the CFO with this same logic that the analysis was incomplete or in some way incorrect. If this can be explained to the CFO then it could likely be accepted by the CFO and the analysis could be updated and corrected. If the CEO is not capable of explaining where the analysis is incorrect, but just believes the opposite is true, then it would be best that they note this difference of opinion, but since it cannot be argued or proved correct or incorrect, it would be likely better to proceed as planned by the CFO. Then, if the CEO turned out to be right, he could argue that the next few times, that the default decision would be the CEO. A good CEO will wait until the CFO has made one mistake while the CEO had recommended a different course. Then they would be right in using that fact to override the CFO the next few times. If the CEO regularly disagrees with the CFO and the CEO is usually wrong, the decent CEO will stop disagreeing with the CFO and start to agree with them almost by default. The situation can change once the CFO has made an error. This will ensure the best results and will allow the CEO to disagree with the CFO but only in reasonable circumstances.

This strategy is a good strategy for any staff member that reports to another staff member. The supervisor should respect and trust the work of the staff member being supervised. To ensure that you are not micromanaging that staff member, it is good to give that person most of the decision making power, until they have proven that they do not deserve this power. If they have demonstrated that they regularly make poor decisions, then it is important for you to frequently override their decisions, but if they have a solid history of making the right decisions, then it is in everyone's best interest to delegate a lot of the decision making authority to them.

Mutual Respect

The way this relationship should ideally work is that both respect the work of each other. The CEO should listen to the recommendations of the CFO for the most part. The CEO must understand that the CFO is the expert on the finances and the CEO is not. If the CEO has some concerns with any decision being proposed, he should raise those issues at a meeting between the two of them. This will allow the CFO to provide further information to the CEO if required. If the CEO just cannot see it or just does not believe it, the CEO should state this and still go with the decision, but if it is proven to be the wrong course of action, the CEO would now be in a position to trust his or her instincts and override the CFO in the future. The CEO should understand that if they disagree with the CFO frequently, then there is likely something wrong with the CEO. The CFO has the capabilities in finance and generally, the CEO does not have the same abilities.

Fall into Place

After some time, the CEO will realize that the CFO has made the right decisions and then will trust the CFO much more. The CEO will also begin to understand where it is fine to trust the CFO and on which rare occasions he may want to override the decisions of the CFO. By mostly agreeing with each other, these two major positions of the company will work harmoniously together and this will benefit the company greatly. The best CEOs that I worked with all used this approach, while the worst CEOs that I worked with used a very different approach. The best CEOs led to a very harmonious working relationship where the company flourished and the poor CEOs decided to do things on their own, which lead to disastrous results. The good CEOs built a strong relationship with the CFO and the results were stunning for the company. The poor CEOs did not build a strong relationship, they created a very weak or even harmful relationship, this caused the company to face major issues. The interesting thing is that each of my supervisors that was weak in these areas all had the following characteristics, they could not delegate, they micromanaged everything, they were not competent in their role, this lack of confidence made them unusually defensive and prone to blame others for their mistakes. While my strongest supervisors all were the opposite, they were strong at delegating, they focused on the big picture, they had confidence in their work and they were competent in their role. These supervisors all had success in their role and moved the company forward. The weak supervisors all struggled with their work and usually moved the company in the wrong direction, at best they remained still.

CHAPTER 7 - BOARD & THE CFO

Most companies have the CFO reporting directly to the CEO and sometimes with some oversight with the board or some part of the board. In the ideal situation, the CFO should be primarily reporting to the board and have oversight by the CEO. Most companies get this wrong, but some are now getting it correct.

Two Critical Roles

The CEO and the CFO are two vital roles for any company, by having the CFO report directly to the CEO, the company is giving too much power to the CEO. This can work well with a CEO with a proven track record for success, but ultimately even if it works well for a while, it is not the ideal situation. A better situation would be the CEO has oversight for the day to day matters but for large matters such as performance reviews, the Board should be the major player. The CEO should be a major contributor to the performance reviews of the CFO, but should not be the sole person to make the final judgment.

Good Governance

For good governance, it is wise to keep the reporting lines of the CFO and CEO separate with some oversight but not a direct reporting line. This will ensure that the CFO has direct contact with the Board and will be able to bring matters up to the board where there are major differences of opinion. It will prevent situations where the CEO just overrides the decision of the CFO. This will force the two major positions to work better with each other and foster strong relations. Without having the CFO report to the Board, the CEO will be able to ensure that the CFO fully listens to their view, even if the CEO is incorrect. It will also mean that for any disagreement there is, that the CFO will not have an independent third party to assess the situation. In this case, likely, the CEO will simply ignore the CFO.

By correcting the reporting lines, the CEO will think twice or three times before simply disagreeing with the CFO. If the CEO is going to disagree with the CFO on a major decision, they will know that it will need to go through the board to make a decision. This would not make either the CEO or the CFO look good, but if the CFO is correct and the CEO is wrong, it will particularly make the CEO look bad. Should the board decide with the CEO and it turns out later that it was the wrong decision, then they will lose faith in the CEO and it will be very likely the last time that the CEO will disagree with the CFO, at least the last time they will go to the Board, the CEO will understand that by making a mistake the last time, the Board will likely decide in favor of the CFO this time around. If the arrangement is that the CFO reports to the CEO, it is very possible that even though the CFO may have the right advice, the CEO would be free to choose the wrong option. There is nothing to prevent the CEO to repeat this pattern over and over again. The only people that are aware of this disagreement would be the CEO and the CFO, in cases where the CFO reports directly and solely to the CEO. In essence, this situation can turn two strong opinions into one opinion. That would not be ideal for the company.

Direct Reporting Line to the Board
The most positive result would be where the Board directly

supervises the CFO, then any major disagreement between the CFO and CEO will be presented to the board for consultation. This is good for the company and both the CEO and CFO. If the CFO is usually correct, it will force the CEO to listen to the CFO more often, to avoid coming to the board and being proven to be incorrect. If on the other hand, the CEO is mostly correct, it will also reduce the number of times this is elevated to the Board and the CFO will listen more to the decisions of the CEO. This will have the benefit of ensuring that the relationship between the two is enhanced and will ensure better cooperation between the two. At the onset of this situation, there could be some adjustment for both individuals, especially if they are more used to having the CFO directly report to the CEO.

Hybrid Solution

There is a hybrid situation and that is where the CFO reports directly to the CEO but has an indirect reporting line to the Board. This solution can work, but oftentimes the direct reporting line to the CEO plays the dominant factor and it overrides the indirect reporting line to the Board. There are times where this does work and only major disagreements are brought to the board. For this situation to work efficiently, there must be mechanisms in place where it is agreed, when the Board will be brought into the equation. It must be understood by both the CFO and the CEO that from time to time, for a major disagreement, the Board will be the arbitrator of the situation. It cannot be seen by the CEO as a threat or it cannot be misunderstood as a lack of trust or lack of respect for the authority of the CEO. This, in theory, sounds possible, but in reality, this is much harder to achieve and the end effect is usually the same as a direct reporting line to the CEO. Hence, to get this correct, the relationship between the Board and the CFO should be a direct reporting line, but not a direct reporting line for day to day activities. The day to day activities should be overseen by the CEO, but for all major aspects of function, performance reviews, and other matters this should be managed by the Board. In the ideal situation, the Board will play less and less role on this oversight and a better relationship will be created between the CFO and CEO.

A company needs to decide whether they want to have two strong voices deciding on how to run the company or one. In most situations, the two voices would produce a better outcome. It can be left between the two parties on how to settle major disputes before it needs to get to the Board, but should a decision be so wrong by either party, then the other can raise it to the board. This will mean more board involvement but it will prevent a lot of bad mistakes from taking place which could result in irreversible consequences to the company.

Most Common Reporting Line
In short, the most common reporting line for a CFO is to the CEO, but as companies grow in size some are moving towards the Board having direct oversight of the CFO. This is the ideal approach is it takes away the possibility of the CEO creating a one-man show. This is particularly important where the CEO is not that capable and has tendencies to make the wrong decisions. If the company has the CFO report to the CEO directly and the CEO is ill-equipped to lead the company properly, the CEO will make many errors and there will be little room for the CFO to prevent the CEO from making these errors. This would be the worst of all possibilities. You would have a competent CFO and an incompetent CEO who just overrides the recommendations of the CFO. There would be no recourse for the CFO. They may go to the Board, but that may be seen as going behind the back of the CEO. This is a no-win situation for both the company and the CFO. By having the CFO report directly to the Board, this situation can be almost eliminated. The Board will be able to quickly see that the decisions made by the CEO are incorrect and those decisions are now harming the company. This would have one of two effects, the first most likely effect is that the CEO would quickly start listening to the advice of the strong CFO or the Board would tire of

the CEO making the wrong decisions and decide that it is time for the CEO to leave. In either case, there is a dramatic improvement in the operations and results of the company.

Not all companies have a strong enough Board to accomplish this, but at a minimum, this should be attempted. Any company that wants strong results and good governance should at a minimum request joint oversight of the CFO by the Board and CEO. Where the majority of the daily functions of the CFO reports directly to the CEO but the CFO has some direct reporting functions to the board. This would be the second most ideal position.

In summary, for the company to ensure the strongest results and the best good governance, the CFO should report directly to the board, with an indirect reporting line to the CEO. It should be clear that major issues of dispute normally would go to the board for clearance. It is also clear that the performance review of the CFO is to be performed by the board with input from the CEO. This will allow a strong separation from the two roles and prevent the CEO from taking over the role of the CFO and forcing them to agree with their decisions, whether they are right or wrong.

If this ideal situation is not possible, then the less ideal situation of a direct reporting line to the CEO but with some oversight of the Board is also positive, but it is far less positive from the ideal situation. This would result in decent results and while good governance would not be obtained, at least some good governance would be achieved.

The situation to avoid is where the CEO has complete oversight over the work and review of the CFO with no oversight from the board. This could result in very poor results for the company and will result in poor governance overall.

CHAPTER 8 - POTENTIAL EFFECTS CFO ON THE BUSINESS

"The CFO used to be the person in the organization who knew the most about the financial state of the business and could choose how to share this knowledge. Today, the CFO needs to be more transparent and make financial information available to other departments so they can operate more efficiently, make decisions quicker, and do the right thing sooner. CFOs are challenged with turning the numbers into something meaningful. You need to be able to derive insights and deliver information to the rest of the organization. The integrity, flexibility, and speed of that information enable your management and staff to more effectively manage the business."

— CHRIS PASS, CFO OF JOHN MUIR HEALTH

A strong CFO can have a positive effect on all aspects of a company and can be well worth their weight in gold. The strong CFO will be able to provide invaluable analysis and reports to the CEO so that the best decisions are made. The CEO must understand that they have a solid CFO, this will create and foster a strong relationship.

Leadership

By providing leadership to the finance teams the CFO will have the most significant effect on the direction and success of all finance teams. This will improve their motivation and improve their effectiveness. With the leadership from the CFO, the finance teams will be directed to work on the reports that deliver the strongest and most actionable results. This will allow managers in other units to rely on the work of the finance teams and ensure that the most logical decisions are being made. It is critical for success that all units can rely on the financial accuracy of the financial reports that they are provided. Managers and the operational teams must have the reports they need and have these reports on a timely basis, these reports must contain actionable data.

The CFO will be able to create strong partnerships from the finance side to all other units across the company. This is critical to success. The other teams must know that they can rely on the finance team and also ask them for additional information as required. If one unit does not feel that the reports are meeting their needs, it is critical that this is addressed immediately and not to let these feelings fester. It may be that the manager is correct or it may be that they are not correct, but the first thing that needs to be done is have a dialogue so that both sides can understand what is going on and whether some additional reports are required. It may be that the information is there but the teams are not sure how to use this information. If this is the case, there should be some additional training given by the finance teams on how to best use this information. The situation may call for reports that are not possible to prepare. If this is the case, the reason for this situation must be made clear and potentially other solutions may be required. There are often situations when financial data is entered into the software, a certain type of report was not thought about. Then later, it may be required, but if the data is not segmented in such a way to allow for this report, it would be very costly and difficult to deliver such a report with accuracy. This should be explained up front and made clear that if such reports are required it will require a re-inputting of a lot of financial transactions and it will come at a significant cost in manpower, resources, and time. If this occurs at the start of the year, it may not be too difficult to redo the data from the start of the year, but if this change is required towards the end of the year, it may be best to wait until next year to deliver this information.

Reporting and their Intended Purpose

Newly requested reports may also not serve the intended purpose from the requestor. If this is the case, it is necessary to explain why the report that is being requested will not meet the perceived gap. It is important to have a frank discussion on this and understand why the person has this point of view and why the person has got it wrong. The most important thing is that a frank and open discussion is needed to ensure that both sides are understood. It could also occur that because of this discussion another report that is already available may meet the client's needs. This can then be shared with them to find out how the report can be adapted to fully support their needs.

By meeting the needs of the departments and divisions that require the financial data, every department and division will improve in their performance. They will be able to make more informed decisions and be able to make decisions more quickly. This would have a significant and positive effect on the whole company. As well, the finance team will be able to assist these leaders to develop reports that they feel they need but are not getting. This will further improve their efficiency and improve the partnership between finance and other teams.

Effective Teams

Finance teams will be highly functioning under the direction of a strong CFO and morale will be highest. By ensuring the proper staff is being recognized by their work, this will motivate staff to do better, since they know if they perform better it will be recognized and equally they understand that if they perform poorly that will reflect on their grading and their potential promotion within the finance units. In addition, as the finance teams are gaining respect among other units, this will drive their results further. This results in a positive cycle where better results mean more recognition, further recognition drives a stronger attitude and better morale, which then leads to better results. This is a strong indication of a good CFO when his teams are accomplishing more, then that is a result of good leadership, conversely when his teams are failing this is usually a result of poor leadership. This can result quickly in a vicious circle or a catch-22.

External Relations

External relations are critical to the success of a CFO. The CFO must be able to build trust with external partners such as the external auditors, exchange commissions, the shareholders, prospective investors, banking institutions, and many others. By fostering strong partnerships and building trust, the CFO will be able to ensure that the rates on bank loans are at the most preferable terms possible. They should be able to discuss and convince external auditors of their accounting treatment should there be any disagreement and meet all the needs of compliance for SEC regulations. The financial projections made by the company must be achievable and reasonable. If the CFO is not able to justify the rationale for their estimates and this information is not widely trusted, this will have a negative effect on the share price. The CFO must be able to develop and nurture strong partnerships and instill trust.

CEOs will need to rely on their CFO to help them make the best decisions. If a CEO does not trust their CFO, this is a recipe for a disaster. A CEO who does not trust his CFO is rarely able to manage a good company. Generally one is at fault, it is either the CFO or the CEO who is wrong. When there is a disagreement, it is usually the CEO that is wrong and usually because there was something that the CEO did not understand from the CFO. Generally, the CFO takes more of an objective view of things and the CEO takes more of a subjective view. Their work does overlap significantly but what got them to their position today is by being one of the best in their field. The CFO who is providing information to the CEO is providing information from his turf, from his specialty. If the CEO is telling the CFO that their data or their analysis is incorrect, then nine times out of ten, it is the CEO who got it wrong. The same is true if the CEO would present their data to the CFO and the CFO would disagree with them, then nine times out of ten the CFO would be wrong. It is similar to having a professional basketball player and a professional hockey player when the professional hockey player talks about hockey and the professional basketball player disagrees, generally speaking, the basketball player will be wrong about hockey. The reverse is also true if the pro hockey player disagrees with the pro basketball player on the topic of basketball, then nine times out of ten the hockey player will be wrong. They both know and understand sports but one is specialized in one sport and the other in another sport. The same is true of the CEO and CFO, both excel at business, but one focuses on one strength and the other comes from another strength. It is fine that they disagree, but regular disagreements will generally point to a CEO who is wrong. The CFO also often reports to the CEO, so they would not be in a position to disagree with their boss. They would understand that disagreeing with the person that you are reporting to is not wise. They would also likely understand that the CEO understands certain topics very well and can be seen as an expert on those, hence, another reason the CFO will not disagree with the CEO on topics that the CEO is the expert. For this reason, a disagreement based on what the CEO says is far less likely. Hence, most disagreements are based on the CEO not agreeing with the analysis from the CFO. In my experience, most CEOs that I worked with fully agreed with me. A colleague, had one CEO who agreed with him fully for one year and his company was very successful. Then the following year the

CEO started disagreeing with him on most things, the company quickly took a sharp turn for the worse. The CEO had decided that he would listen to another executive instead of the CFO. My colleague soon left. The company has been and continues to struggle. The future financial viability remains in question. It is not a good situation when the CEO disagrees with the CFO and especially deadly when the CFO is correct. In these situations, I can attest that 90% of the time the CFO is correct. If however, the CEO agrees with the CFO for the majority of the time and picks the odd time then, in this situation the CEO is more likely to be correct because they are picking and choosing when to disagree, but for the most part, they are agreeing with their CFO.

Right or Wrong?

There is another clear cut way to tell who is correct, if the company is failing and the CEO is not listening to the CFO, then the CEO should start to listen to the CFO. The CFO would be right and the CEO wrong. If on the other hand, the company is flourishing and the CEO is not listening to the CFO then it is likely that the CEO is correct and the CFO is wrong. If they are not disagreeing and the company is doing poorly then both are wrong, while in most situations the company is doing as expected or slightly better and they are not in disagreement, in these cases both are correct.

In a well-functioning company, the CFO will have a positive influence over the CEO and the company will head in a direction that is agreed to by both. This situation provides the greatest likelihood of success.

Strong leadership qualities are necessary, they can assist to drive finance teams for better results, help lead the CEO, and help external parties. These leadership qualities are a critical strength of a CFO. When done right, the whole company is motivated to move in the correct direction and make the right choice. As well, external parties perceive the company in a better light and understand the financial situation of the company, this allows external parties to make more informed investment decisions.

CHAPTER 9 – STRUGGLING CFO

There are several reasons why a CFO may be struggling. One of the most common reasons for a struggling CFO is that they do not have the external prerequisites to be successful. As described earlier if the CFO does not have a solid CEO, a solid Board to back them up, strong financial teams, or a company that is performing well, the CFO may be struggling in that environment. Certain prerequisites can be improved over time through the work of the CFO and certain prerequisites may not be improved upon simply by the work of the CFO, but may require the assistance from the Board or may take a lot longer to achieve.

The CFO may also be struggling due to internal issues, they may not have the personal prerequisites to become a successful CFO. If the CFO was successful in one institution they do likely have the internal prerequisites. But if never successful, or it is their first time being a CFO, then if they are not able to master the role of CFO it may be that they lack certain internal prerequisites for being a successful CFO.

Business Acumen
The first key strength a CFO should have is strong business acumen and strong business sense. The CFO should be able to quickly

analyze a business and find out areas that work and areas that are struggling. Without this ability, the CFO will not be able to direct their attention to the areas of the business that need it and away from areas that do not need it. The CFO will not be efficient and due to that, they will not be successful. This also requires a very strong understanding of financial reports and having strong analytical skills. The CFO, without this strength, will only be able to continue on the work of their predecessors but will not be able to drive new paths. This may be successful for a short period but it will not be successful in the long run. Hence, a company that is running well for many years may continue to run well with a new CFO but in time, the operations may change and things may start to fall apart if the new CFO is not able to address these issues and resolve them swiftly, then the company will start to decline slowly and then decline quite rapidly. This would be the case of where a CFO is lacking certain skills but has taken over a well-run company. Then when the company starts to fail the CFO will not have the ability to solve these issues. This is the point where a strong CEO would be required to see that there is a problem and there should be a removal of the CFO. The CFO should be presented with the problem and should be given the chance to identify and recommend corrections to resolve the issue or issues, if they cannot do so, then it would be time to search for a more qualified CFO.

Leadership

Leadership skills are an important prerequisite for a CFO to possess. The CFO must be capable to develop a strong vision of what the best possible future can be. This would be the first step in being a strong leader, that would be knowing what to do and when to do it. In other words, figuring out what the best solution is or coming up with the best vision for the way forward, is the first necessary ingredient to being a strong leader. The next step is to be able to explain that vision and get buy-in from others. It is one thing to have a good vision, but if you cannot convince others that your vision is correct, then being correct has very little value. Hence, the second skill required is being able to influence others to share in your vision or to accept your vision. These two ingredients are the main ingredients for being a great leader. The next ingredient would be being able to manage the implementation of that vision. One may argue that this belongs to management and not being a leader. The reality is both ways of looking at it are correct, but if you cannot effectively get the teams to implement your vision, then your leadership will not matter. As such, we will keep it as an important ingredient to leadership. You have to be able to come up with the right vision, you need to be able to influence others to get your vision accepted, and you need to be able to get the teams to implement your vision. After these three goals are achieved, you then need to see the results of these changes. It is important to be able to measure quickly and reliably, whether these actions result in any improvements or any changes that are worse. Then, one can see if the vision was successful. When we look at what makes a good leader, there are many factors that one may think about, such as, a good speaker, a good writer, the ability to come up with great ideas, the ability to motivate teams, and many other factors, but really it can be resolved by one simple area, the ability to achieve positive results. A good leader must have all of the above to achieve strong results. It would also be hard to say that someone is a good leader if they have not achieved great results.

If we look at a CFO that has all the abilities to influence, manage teams, ensure that teams are properly motivated and enthusiastic for results but comes up with the wrong vision. Then the result of this would be that the wrong vision would be agreed upon as the way forward, it would be implemented and it would prove a failure since it was the wrong vision. This person may look like a leader as he can influence people and get teams motivated, but without knowing the proper solution to implement, all that this individual has done would be to waste time and resources. Overall, this person would not be a good leader. As well, due to the failure, this person would now have a lot more difficulty in convincing people to go along with their vision the next time around.

Another example would be someone that can come up with the right vision but may not have the ability to influence the teams to accept their vision. In this case, the vision would never be implemented and the result would be a failure. There may be some people that agree with the vision but not enough to move forward. This would be a net failure. In this case, the CFO would not be a strong leader, but at least the CFO would know that they need to focus on their skills of influencing people. It may become known that the person was right in the end, and perhaps the next time around this person will have greater influence.

In essence, all three traits are required to be a successful leader, coming up with the right vision, the ability to influence others to see that your vision is the correct one to follow, and being able to direct teams to implement your vision. When the leader can accomplish all three of these successfully and then the results are there to show that the vision was correct, then this leader can truly be seen as a strong leader. Some people may suggest that you can be a strong leader without generating strong results, I would disagree with this concept with one caveat. If the strong results were averted due to a reason beyond their control and beyond their ability to project, then even with a lack of results, the person can potentially be a strong leader. In essence, one could say the proof is in the pudding. Hence, if you have a strong leader there should also be a history of strong results. I would argue, and many agree, that you cannot be a strong leader without strong successes, it cannot be every time that a leader runs with their vision there is something that occurs beyond their control that stops them from having success.

Building Teams

The CFO must be capable of building strong teams to support their work. The critical team would be the finance team. If the

CFO is not able to properly motivate teams and staff within those teams, then the CFO will be struggling. Part of the ability to build strong teams would be to share a strong vision with the teams, but there is far more to it than just a vision.

To build a strong team, the CFO must be able to assess where the team is successful and where the team is struggling. Being able to read a person is a critical factor to success. There are going to be people on a team who will try to distort the truth. There will be others that will try to shift the blame and there will be others that work very hard but may lack certain training to be successful. The CFO must be able to rid out the bad influences in a team. There are always certain people on a team that may cause the team more damage than provide value. It is critical to focus on these individuals and either get them to quickly change their way of operating or to get them off the team. There is nothing more destructive to a team than a person who is purposely dragging his feet while others are working hard. This can create an atmosphere of resentment and demotivate good staff. A person might think, why should I work hard when that person is doing nothing and gets the same treatment as I do. If you cannot identify the bad apples on your team, then it will be very difficult to create strong teams.

Motivation

A CFO must understand what motivates people and what demotivates people. It is also important to understand that every person is different and what motivates one may demotivate another. Ensure that the motivation is in line with the people who respond well to that motivation. For example, some people may love the chance to attend a new training, and others may find that this is too much additional work for them. It is important to know who responds well and who does not. It is also important to know when someone is deserving of recognition for their good work and when someone does not deserve this recognition.

Developing your Team

You need to be able to assess why a person is succeeding and why a person is struggling. If a person is struggling due to a lack of training, then it may well be worth the efforts to get that training for this individual. This is particularly true for the person who works hard and has a great attitude, but is not excelling due to a lack of training in a certain area. Then investing in this person would make good sense, especially where the benefits of their improved work will exceed the costs. It is also good to recognize hard work and a good attitude, this will motivate others that it is not only about results but also about the attitude that matters. It is one thing to have success but also good to have highly motivated people around you. There is a potential to have a highly skilled person who delivers well but is not giving it all, they may have a negative attitude. It would be important to identify this person and find out what does motivate them. Perhaps the job they are doing is too simple for them, it would be wise to give them further challenges and see if they can deliver. This person with the right incentives may be able to do much more. By finding out what motivates different types of people you can ensure that your teams are delivering to their potential. This is a key element needed for a successful CFO.

Without developing successful teams around the CFO, they will not be able to achieve the results they aspire to achieve. Hence, this is a necessary ability to have. The strong CFO must know how to develop and motivate teams to success and ensure they are delivering the right results at the right time.

CHAPTER 10 – REPORTING

One cannot underestimate the importance of reporting in the role of a CFO and the success of any company. A company that has a great reporting system that delivers important information promptly is one that will have a great advantage. A company, a CFO, and a CEO cannot function properly without getting financial reports to them promptly. It would be like driving with your eyes closed. You need to be able to see where you are going and see when you are heading in the wrong direction. If you cannot determine these things very quickly then it will be that much more costly to make the corrections later. The ability to make the right choices as early as possible or make corrections swiftly can easily be the difference from a thriving company to a struggling company.

New CFO

Whenever a new CFO joins a company, one critical step is evaluating the current reporting system. The reports should be able to inform you if you are meeting your targets or not. The reports should have a list of key performance indicators (KPI) that are being tracked. It is important to ensure that the KPIs are fully inclusive, in other words, there are no KPIs that are missing. The KPIs that do exist should be relevant and should be comprehensive. It is often the case that certain KPIs are missing and could sum up the situation better than other existing KPIs do. Hence, a review of KPIs are necessary from time to time. This review may not be required every quarter but there should be a review each year, at a minimum.

Management should be able to tell which areas of the business are improving, which are standing still and which are falling behind. Then after this, resources could be allocated accordingly. A critical area is being able to compare estimates, budgets, and forecasts with actual data. If a company is projecting $120 M in sales and is expecting this amount to be distributed evenly throughout the year, then there should be alarm bells ringing if the first month only has $6 M in sales. It is critical to find out the reason why the estimates were not met, to justify these reasons, and to come up with a correction. The worst situation is that the projections would need to be lowered, however, given a situation where there is no way to meet the targets, then this is the only option available. It is far better to make these adjustments earlier than later. If the CFO was the one that prepared these estimates in the first place, then he needs to figure out why his estimates were so far off. This should be extremely rare but it might be more common in the case of an outgoing CFO with an incoming CFO who has inherited those projections. It would be his duty to highlight that there are some issues with the projections and that they are getting updated corrections by the close of business today, if possible.

ERP System

The ERP system must be capable of providing all the necessary reports and must function very well. There is nothing worse for a CFO to have an ERP system where the reports are not reliable. These issues could be related to the way the data was imported or could be that the ERP itself has some bugs that have not yet been corrected. These must be corrected right away. Having an ERP system that is reliable and setting up the reports that are required is tantamount for success. A strong CFO will always be looking for ways to improve the system and automate reports. When looking at sales data it is important to have this data daily and up to date, as changes here could have huge effects. When making changes to a sales campaign you want to ensure that you can get immediate feedback on results. If you are not seeing these results reflected in your sales you need to adjust the sales campaign or fix it so that you can get your intended results. To be effective, having immediate and reliable data that you can act on is instrumental to success.

Assessing Current Reports

Being able to assess whether your reports are sufficient or lacking is a necessary strength for any successful CFO and business. If your reports are lacking in some way and you are not aware that they are lacking, then you will only find out when it is too late or when you have already suffered much damage. Being able to identify potential risks and being able to create reports that can monitor that risk and provide a warning when this risk is growing is necessary for maintaining success.

The company may be performing well today but if there are risks that are growing in the background and these risks are not being noticed by the CFO, the CEO, or the management of the company, then it will be negatively affected by this situation sooner than later. This is where a good risk management team and function are critical. Are there certain competitors that are gaining on your market share? Are there certain products that can potentially make your product obsolete? As in the case with Blockbuster and Netflix. These risks should always be measured and evaluated. The minute a company believes that all is well is the moment that one of these risks will present themselves. Your reports must track these risks and be able to measure these risks. This is the only way that it will be on everyone's radar each month. Having this data will allow a company to take alternative steps that it may not have done naturally.

Small Oversights can turn to Big Problems
Sometimes a major oversight in the part of the company can cause a total collapse of the company as in the case of Blockbuster and other times it does not cause a collapse but a huge opportunity is missed. When IBM was looking for its operating system, they came to Bill Gates and famously agreed that Microsoft could retain the rights to their software, because, in IBM's words, the money is in the hardware, not the software. This wrong way of thinking was the mistake that caused Bill Gates to become one of the richest people on the planet. There are blunders and there are major blunders, these errors would both fall in the latter category.

It is critical to look at technology for where it is going and not only for where it is today. It is also important to understand every related business that affects your business or is affected by your business. Today an understanding of the internet and smartphone capabilities is a must, however, one must understand where we are moving with artificial intelligence, where we are moving with globalization, and where we are moving with regards to data and its ownership. We are likely soon to have self-driving cars and trucks. Will that affect your business positively or negatively? Work that we do manually may soon become more automated. How can we ensure that our business is prepared for that and benefits from that?

Where are we Heading?

The issue of where we are and where we are heading is not only critical to businesses but also critical to people who are entering the workplace or in school. Parents need to think about what kind of work should their children be entering. The way that technology is moving would indicate that people should be looking at being more of an entrepreneur or focusing on areas that artificial intelligence will not be a major competitor. If we look at Lee Se-Dol, the best human at the game Go, which is considered to be one of the most challenging games along with Chess, he has recently retired from the game saying that there is no way that he can compete with Google's Go computer. For the past many generations the computer would be in no shape to beat a human in this game and now the best player in the world is giving up because it is impossible to beat this computer. I played a lot of chess while younger and I recall the first computer chess games that came out. They were quite interesting and some were not bad. I was a very strong player and I would play it on the highest level and most always win. It was interesting that at times it would take hours to make one move and it would still lose. The computers today are far better and now I have to concentrate to beat the computers and at higher levels, they have a better chance of winning than I do. The best chess player in the world has also been beaten by Deep Blue, the famous computer chess system that beat Gary Kasparov. Competing with computers and artificial intelligence will only get worse.

There is a bright side to artificial intelligence, do not try to compete against it but use it to your advantage at work. Artificial intelligence has many weaknesses, it is not very creative and will be a long way away from running a business. Use this to your advantage. Looking at how the markets will change when there is more automation and how to ensure a good customer response is key. Recently having visited Japan and saw a few hotels where they have robots check you in was quite interesting. Think ahead and use this for your business.

Artificial Intelligence

As part of your reporting, you should always put artificial intelligence or technology as both a risk and an opportunity for most if not all businesses. A business can become obsolete due to technology very fast if they are not staying ahead of the curve. Your reporting should not become complacent. The challenge here is that technology is moving very quickly, one may not have expected the internet to explode as fast as it did. If we look at the Sony Walkman, in the day that was the height of technology and was one of the only ways that you could listen to music, while out in public or taking a bus. Then came the Sony Diskman and that technology was far greater. Then the iPod and iPhone completely changed the whole situation. So the question is how do you get your reporting to track competition and upcoming technological advancement threats. This is challenging to do. If you wait to track the actual data it will be too late. Hence, the moment that you have data showing that you are losing out to another technology it is already too late. You may measure a small increase today, but the huge increase in that new technology is only weeks or months away and there is no time to restructure your business to compete. This is where traditional reporting does not help cover this risk. If the technology was advancing slowly, then the traditional reports would be able to give you a fair warning, however, technology has not advanced slowly since 1980, and it is speeding up each year. In this case, the usual rules do not apply, usually one looks to reporting based on quantitative data and qualitative data, while both are important it is usually the quantitative data that plays the greater lead. In the case of looking for risks of future technological advancements, the reverse is true, it is generally based on both quantitative and qualitative data but the qualitative should play a stronger role. It would seem that Blockbuster focused solely on quantitative data but did not consider the qualitative data. Netflix was a competitor but they were nowhere near close to competing with Blockbuster at that time. When they realized the truth, it was too late.

A critical function in reporting is surveying the actual risks, potential risks, and future risks that a company is facing. Traditionally, companies have focused on risks that they are facing today and put some effort into potential risks but have not put in the time to measure and address these potential future risks. We have seen this in some major examples and will continue to see this tomorrow. Almost no company is immune to these risks. The best companies have diversified their operations so that if they become obsolete in one area, they still have ten other effective business lines that will continue. This is a good strategy and shows why certain companies like Sony, Phillips, General Electric, and others are immune to competition. As well, there are certain companies like Coke or Pepsi, that are less affected by technology, hence, this risk will not affect them that much. A much better tasting cola may come along, but after over a hundred years, this is very unlikely, as well, should they be losing market share, they can adapt in time. Their main risk may come with regards to health, as more and more people are turning to healthier alternatives, they may need to adapt but this may come in the next 50 years or longer. There will also be clear signs and they will be able to adapt. Perhaps they will create a healthy coke option, healthier than Coke Light or Coke Zero. Coke is not at any risk any time soon.

Hence, while reporting is critical to help you find out where you are going today and where you are heading tomorrow, it is also critical to find out which risks you may be facing in the future.

CHAPTER 11 - CFO & THE FINANCE TEAM

"Things like team-building that used not to happen, that's going to be built in. It's not my style to sit in my office; I will go to where they are and engage them. You want to develop their communication skills. You want to emphasize the importance of having good interpersonal skills with your fellow stakeholders and other departments. Part of my job is really to coach."

— RAYMOND YEO, CFO OF EPSILON

The successful CFO will need to be able to lead and manage diverse teams, the one team that plays a major role in his or her success would be the finance team. Being one person, the CFO cannot perform all the financial functions of a large organization. When the company is run and managed by one person then this is fine, but after it gets larger, it will require a dedicated CFO. The finance team will be the most important for the CFO to lead and manage well. If the CFO cannot provide a clear vision to their finance team and have that team meet those challenges then he or she is not going to be a successful CFO.

Visionary

Providing a vision to the finance team is a critical starting point for any CFO. With this vision, the finance team will understand why they are doing what they are doing. Without explaining this vision and getting buy-in from the team this leader will have a hard time succeeding. The vision must be understandable, reasonable, and achievable to be accepted. If any of these three are missing the vision will not be a success. The vision must also map out the steps to success in a somewhat concrete manner, but the full details would not be necessary to start. A vision of improving the ERP system may be a good vision, but if you do not explain what it will change to and how that change will be implemented, it will not be widely accepted. A CFO that is looking at a team that has been using an underperforming reporting system will need to explain to them how this can be improved upon. It is important to do this reasonably. You do not want to criticize the old system, this will have the effect of splitting the team up to those who support the old way of doing things and those that may support the new way. You should compliment the old system but explain that with the changing times we need to also change and so does our reporting system.

Sharing your Vision

You must explain your vision and why the vision is right for today and tomorrow. You must allow a dissenting view to be heard but not to run away with the crowd. If you know that your vision is correct, then you should not worry about hearing an opposing view. You should make it clear that the time for making a counter-argument is now, but once a decision is made, there will be no time to discuss the merits of the old ways or the new ways. If there is overwhelming support for your view and a few hold-outs with a dissenting view. The best way forward is to end the discussion and table the majority view but state that you will reach out to those with a different viewpoint to investigate why. It is important to do so with an open mind and listen to their opinions, it can be one on one or allow many of them together to hear their side. You can then ask them to get together and prepare their three strongest concerns against the proposed changes. Give them a day or so to put it together and then take the time to review each point with them after, fully reviewing it first. With each of the three major concerns, you should be able to mitigate the issue, explain the difference or agree that this is an issue but look at alternate ways to move forward.

Allow Opposing Views

Often when a group is asked to put the top three problems they have with a proposed solution, there is little consensus of what are the top three issues. This will illustrate to the team that there are no glaring issues and the issues that they are bringing up are rather small or easily addressed. Often, the group may decide to bring up three issues, but agree that these can be handled, thus taking the burden off of your shoulders. This is an excellent way of putting out what could have turned into a fire. It is also a way for the team to vent their frustrations and create a document that may make you reconsider the proposed solution. If the document is not convincing enough but still presented. You can then start from agreeing with their concerns but show how their concerns are being dealt with or not being dealt with. If the concerns that they raise are valid and do cause you to re-evaluate the situation, then tell them thanks for their hard work and you will need to reconsider certain aspects to take these concerns into account. This situation is possible but not that likely. If none of the concerns warrants a rethink but do warrant an explanation of why the issue is either not important or will be taken up later, then thank the team for their time and devotion, but after reading your concerns, it is clear to me that these concerns are already met or will be met, as such, we will be proceeding with the approved plan. Let them know that if they still have any concerns they can meet with you one on one, but your time is very limited. Let them know that you also expect them to be fully on board with the plan, but we will tabulate your concerns and should any of these concerns be an issue after three years of implementation then you will apologize to each of them. But right now, you do not want to hear anything more on the topic, unless you would like to discuss this one on one with me.

In this scenario, you are ready to move on with the whole team behind your vision. Some may be wary of the change and hence why they are reluctant but soon they will see the benefits of the change. The important thing is that now the whole team is behind you and you also allowed a dissenting view and gave them time to make their case. The dissenting view may also provide you information that you need to slightly change your proposal to ensure the concern is addressed. This is progress and if you are clearly showing that the concern that was raised was important enough to warrant a slight alteration of the proposal, this will allow the full team to be happy with the way forward. What you should not do is just present them your solution and not listen to any of their ideas. Some "leaders" feel this is the best way, this is incorrect, listening to as many points of view as possible is the right way and the true leader does this. When a decision has been made, then it is no longer the time for second-guessing that decision.

Segregation of Duties

You must have clear segregation of duties and responsibilities for every member on your finance team. You need to ensure that the financial analysts know what they are supposed to do and who they report to, just as the financial reporting teams must know what they are supposed to do. The finance team should be broken down into separate units that take care of separate functions. Each of the units should report to a manager and a few managers should report to one director, then each director should report to the CFO. You can structure the team by different titles but for large teams, you need to have different groups or units that each cover separate functions. It is critical that one group or unit only covers one set of functions and that there do not exist two separate units that cover the same set of functions. If you do not have a clear divide between functions, then you may run into a situation where both teams are treating this responsibility as theirs, this may cause turf wars and hostility among the teams. It needs to be very clear where there is any doubt. This will allow for proper motivation and take away any uncertainty. If the function is successful or not, you also know which unit to congratulate or to get them to work better. A finance team that does not have a clear distinction from their duties will not be successful and will not be properly motivated. The strong CFO will need to make sure that these functions are set apart very clearly and which unit is responsible for which function or functions. A strong CFO and leader will be able to make this very clear to the team.

Job Responsibilities

Just as the responsibilities of each unit must be made very clear from the top, the managers of each unit must also make very clear how the roles are divided within that team. You do not want to have mini turf wars within finance units and you do not want to have staff who are unsure of their duties. There may be staff that has the same functions and responsibilities, this is fine, as long as it is clear, but for those that have different responsibilities, the difference should also be very clear. The CFO should understand when units are not delivering and why they are not delivering. It could be that a unit is not delivering as expected due to an unclear division of duties. This should be addressed as soon as possible.

By having a clear and transparent breakdown of responsibilities within units and staff, this will go a long way to assist with the proper motivation of teams and staff members. It will ensure that there are few turf wars and ensure that teams work together rather than work apart. This is critical to get this right and where strong leadership is required to correct any issues here.

Clear Reporting Lines

There must be a well-defined reporting line in place. All staff should know who their supervisor is and who their secondary supervisor is if there is a secondary one. There may be specific projects that blur these lines or are exceptions to these reporting lines, but apart from special projects, all staff must follow the correct reporting lines. The key leader of this is the CFO, one may appreciate the concept of an open door policy. While this, used correctly can be a great way to get further support and get a better understanding of what goes on at the various levels, it is important that this is not being abused. The key problem with an open door policy is that a staff member may describe a situation that he feels his supervisor made an unfair decision. This situation can come in many forms and it may seem very innocuous at first, but it could result in very poor results rather quickly.

The minute that a staff member complains about the decision that a supervisor has taken, it is important that you inform the person, that you may listen to the story but you will not take one action to help him or her. You can explain to the person that there are reporting lines in place and they are there for a reason. If the issue is very serious then it could be brought up to HR, but you are not HR and will not be playing the role of HR. You may say, that before you continue, you must think about the following, are you badmouthing your boss? Is this such a serious issue that you should go to HR with? Or is it an issue that you just want to get off your chest? If it is any of those three issues then I don't need to be aware of it. Is it something that negatively affects your team and have you brought it to the attention of your supervisor? If yes, what was their response? If not, why not? The CFO should recommend to the staff member that they first bring it up to their supervisor before addressing it with you. By doing so, it will show that you fully support the reporting lines and do not want to hear about anything that is between a staff member and their supervisor unless it has large potential consequences. This will also send a message to others that you do not support talking about supervisors behind their backs. You can also suggest that if you feel very strongly about an issue, you are very happy to discuss this with both of them, the staff member and supervisor, after you have first discussed it directly with the supervisor. This allows the supervisor the ability to hear and address the issue if it is an issue.

Support and Enforce Reporting Lines

If leadership does not support both verbally and with actions, the defined reporting lines, then it will become a free for all and any-time someone has a complaint they will come to your door. This is exactly the situation that you do not want to have. This will have the direct effect of reducing the ability of your managers to effectively manage their teams and will have you working over-time to resolve conflicts where they need not escalate to you. If this situation comes to this level, it is because of poor leadership at the top. A poor leader who allows this to occur could ruin it for all the strong leaders that are under the poor leader. If any staff has the feeling that they do not have to listen to their supervisor, if they do not feel like it, this is a recipe for disaster. The problem is that most poor leaders are completely oblivious to their faults and the potential repercussions of certain actions.

Motivation

To properly motivate staff, teams, and leaders within your team, everyone must follow the correct reporting lines. There are a few exceptions to this rule, such as fraud or abuse, but very few other exceptions. Staff should work with their supervisors and super-visors should be fair with their staff. Then, supervisors can ensure that the staff is properly motivated. If a staff member is under-performing, then the supervisor can address that staff member's performance without the staff simply turning and complaining to another supervisor or the CFO.

Staff must have the correct motivation to get the best results. If a staff member performs well but someone else gets credit for that work. This will send the wrong message for motivation. You want to ensure good work is rewarded and poor work is not rewarded. There must be a clear, transparent and objective way to measure staff results and results from units. The evaluation of results should be objective as much as possible with some subjectivity. The overlying driver must be the objective results with the subjective issues adding flavor but not being the major factor. Hence, if a finance staff was supposed to deliver ten reports each month before the seventh of the month, this should be easy to review and evaluate. Did he or she achieve this all the time or only some of the time? It is also important to ensure that if he is not able to deliver the results was it due to his oversight or another person's oversight? For example, if they are supposed to deliver the reports before the 7th of each month, but they are supposed to get the data by the 4th of each month, perhaps their lateness was caused by getting the data late each month. A staff member should only be held responsible for things within their control.

Setting Objectives

Setting the expectations of results must be done very fairly to properly motivate any staff member. The expectations must be achievable, reasonable and measurable, if they are not, then there is a possibility of deeming strong staff as weak and the reverse as well. This will create a lack of motivation across the team and lead to poor results. The strong CFO must work with their leaders and teams and with HR to ensure that this process works smoothly. You want to reward those staff members that deserve it and not those that do not deserve rewarding.

Proper Delegation

To motivate the senior members of your team, it is critical that you have trust in them and that you delegate the duties accordingly. The worst way to treat a strong team member is to micro-manage their work, when they are capable. This is wrong for many reasons, first, it takes a very competent manager and demotivates them. It takes away trust from your critical relationship, by micro-managing a strong team member, you are saying that you do not trust them, either their capabilities or their motivations. As well, you are diverting your precious time to areas where it is not needed and away from areas where it may be needed. This will have the effect of having good staff leave you and you will be left with weaker staff. There are team members who are not as capable and may need some help, in this case, these are the people to give extra time to or micro-manage for a brief period. If you treat strong staff as you do weak staff, this will not properly motivate the stronger staff. You will only be motivating these strong staff to look elsewhere. It will also send a message to the teams that you do not know how to tell the difference from a strongly performing staff member and a poorly performing staff member. No leader, can be a regular micro-manager and also be successful. Micro-managers have not learned to properly delegate tasks and they take them all to themselves. This has the undesired effect of demotivating strong staff and motivating weak staff. In some cases, a strongly performing staff member may be promoted to a leader or worse to a CEO. In some cases, this person was promoted due to his or her fine attention to detail. This may be a strength at a lower level, but it is this exact strength that will quickly turn to your biggest weakness as a leader. You will not know how to delegate and hence, you will not be able to properly motivate your teams. If this person happens to be the CEO, then this will spell havoc for the entire company. People who improve because they have been able to be focused on the details is exactly the person who would not make a good leader and generally end up not making good leaders. The unfortunate truth is that very few people who spent decades focusing on details can change this in a matter of years to become effective leaders. As much as they are aware that this is their weakness, they are still incapable of fixing this.

It is almost like asking the best sumo wrestler in the world to become the best gymnast in one year. By not having the ability to delegate, you will not motivate your teams properly. A critical ability in delegation is understanding who is competent and who is struggling. More support can go to those struggling and more autonomy to those who are performing well is the right formula. By being able to do this naturally, you will be able to properly motivate your teams and give more autonomy to those that can handle it and more support to those that need it. Leadership is required to know the difference and to understand that delegation helps you and your team.

Innovation

Any team that does not innovate is a team that will soon become obsolete. The CFO must ensure that their teams are trying to innovate regularly but not at the expense of getting their work done. They should always be looking for a better way to do things. There is always room for improvement. The important thing here is that these efforts should be limited. While there is always room for improvement and there is always a better way to do things, one must understand that there is a cost-benefit to any change. The minute the benefits exceed the costs, this is when the changes should be implemented and not before. Change is great and it is necessary, but changing major systems each year would cause major disruptions and not yield positive results. There are small innovations that do not have great cost implications but can yield very positive results, this is where the focus should be.

Innovation and thinking outside the box are very important to ensure that teams are properly motivated, if they are supposed to do the same thing for the next twenty years, the motivation levels of the staff in that team may start to erode. This would harm results and it could result in a higher staff turnover rate for that team.

With a strong vision and the correct motivation of teams, units and staff, the CFO can accomplish their vision and ensure a strong and healthy finance team. This is critical for the health of the company and critical for the success of the CFO and the company.

CHAPTER 12 - CFO & THE SHAREHOLDER

Raising money from an IPO is an entirely tactical decision and should be weighed against all the other funding alternatives for private and public companies. Many of the other choices are considerably less expensive than a traditional IPO. If you want to take your company public, that is a different question — one that should not be solely about raising capital.

— BARRY MCCARTHY, CFO OF SPOTIFY

The role of the CFO is a critical role for the existing shareholder and as well for potential shareholders. The CFO will ensure to maximize profitability for the company and this will ensure the best possible growth for stock prices. It will allow for the ability to pay dividends if the Board agrees with the payment of a dividend. In short, it will have a positive and strong effect on the investment that a shareholder has made with the company.

Potential Investors
With potential investors the role is very similar, they must know that they are getting the best financial forecasts and that the esti-

mates are valid and reasonable. If the CFO is overly optimistic in their forecasts, this could have a negative effect once it is shown that the forecast was overly optimistic, this would occur when performance and profitability targets are not met. If a share is trading at $100 with a given set of estimates from the CFO. After some time, those forecasts and estimates will be compared with actual results and these results will either be equal to those estimated, more favorable or less favorable. Hence, let us say that for Q1, the projections were a net profit of $ 50 M, but the actual results showed a value of $ 45 M. This will result in a small decrease in price because the CFO and the company missed the target they had set. Instead, if the results were $55 M, this would result in a small gain in the share price. Any gains in prices are great for those that hold the shares, hence they are great for the existing shareholders. When the results fall short of expectations, this could also trigger the possibility that all future forecasts are likely overstated, this will cause a greater drop in stock prices.

This decrease in stock price may actually be a perfect time for the prospective buyer to buy, but it may also signal that all future estimates should be reduced and thus likely the potential shareholder will refuse to purchase shares. It is critical that the CFO forecasts in a way that the results are likely to occur. The CFO should not be overly optimistic nor overly pessimistic. The goal would be to aim it just right, perhaps giving a buffer of a few percentage points, as getting better results will always result in a slight boost to the stock price and slightly missing the target will likely result in a slight drop in price.

Profitability

The CFO plays a key role in the overall profitability of the company. The stronger the CFO the more likely the company is to have success and make the right decisions that will allow the company to grow. By growing faster a company will be able to drive more profits and take control of more market share. The company will also be able to choose the right investments and choose the rights segments to invest in, this will also cause better growth and profitability. The increased profitability will cause a significant increase in stock prices and with sustained growth the increase in stock prices may be even far greater.

The positive effect on the profitability of a company will have a great effect on the share price and drive the most profit for a shareholder as they will see their investments have a strong return by growing in stock price. If the shareholder decides to sell their shares, they will earn a strong profit on their shares, alternatively, they could decide to hold on to get an even larger gain.

The positive effect that the CFO brings to the profitability of a company will drive a positive effect on the shareholder. The potential shareholder will be able to invest in this company with the understanding that the forecasts presented to the SEC are both reasonable and achievable. The potential investor will benefit as reductions in share prices are far less likely, if the potential investor does not invest, however, they lose any potential benefits of an increasing stock price.

Leadership
By providing leadership to the CEO, the CFO has a direct impact on ensuring the best direction for the company is taken. At a minimum, where the CEO already is very strong, the CFO can provide further support and added confidence to their decisions. The CFO can always support the decision of the CEO or can present another alternative. This relationship and their leadership are key to the overall success of a company. The CFO should be the first one to agree with a good decision and the first one to provide alternatives to potentially poor decisions. This leadership with regards to the CEO is crucial for the success of the company and it could be the difference from a successful company and a poorly performing company.

Leading the finance teams is important to ensure that proper internal controls are maintained. This would include the safeguarding of assets and reducing any potential for fraud. Leadership with the finance teams will also result in stronger reports and better key performance indicators. All teams will have financial data that is more timely, more relevant and better able to make decisions on. This leadership will have a strong impact on the overall success of a company. If the internal controls are weak within a company, it will be very difficult to safeguard assets and prevent fraud. If the financial reports are not at the highest level, it will mean that all departments and business lines or business segments will not be as efficient. This difference alone could be the difference from a thriving and growing company to one that is struggling or failing.

Mergers & Acquisitions

Part of any growth strategy would include the strategy of Mergers & Acquisitions (M&A). The CFO would be critical in deciding which companies are the best priced and best aligned with the direction or growth of the company. This would be very different than just purchasing as an investment, this is purchasing as part of a strategy for growth. If you are selling sneakers, you may want to buy out one of your competitors and take over their market share. This would be a strategic investment. In order to determine whether this acquisition is wise, it is important for the CFO to calculate the costs of that acquisition, the likely estimate of costs to buy and compare it with the added value brought to the company would be necessary. If the costs would be $500 M to acquire the company but the added value to the company would never exceed $ 200 M, then this would not be a good acquisition and the company should not make this acquisition. If the purchase could result in value far greater than the purchase price, then it would make for a good purchase.

There are many types of mergers and acquisitions, if the companies are much the same, this would be called a horizontal merger or acquisition. This would be the case where a shoe company buys another shoe company. If however, the shoe company purchases the company that makes the leather to produce the shoes, then this would be called a vertical merger or acquisition. It is part of the same process but it is at a different point on the supply chain. By being able to guarantee the delivery of goods needed for your product, this will result in stronger value overall. You may also be able to have a competitive edge with your competitors. This could present greater value to each company. Hence by combining the two companies, this is improving the value of both companies. The CFO would need to figure out the costs and whether the merger could be beneficial to both. The company that supplies the goods will benefit by having a guaranteed purchaser and the acquiring company will benefit by having guaranteed materials at the best prices to ensure further success.

Both vertical and horizontal strategies are common and if done correctly they could increase the value of both as a whole. The goal here is that both companies benefit from this arrangement. You do not want the situation where one company benefits but at the expense of the other, as after the acquisition you now own both companies. The goal is to find mergers where the sum of the whole becomes greater than the sum of the parts. Ideally, if you take a $500 M company and add it to another $ 500 M company, you want to have a combined company worth more than $ 1 B. In order to acquire the company worth $ 500 M, you may have to pay about $ 600 M, so you want to ensure the two companies together are worth a minimum of $ 1.1 B and potentially a lot more than that.

Maximizing Value

The shareholders will benefit greatly by having a CFO that is highly successful with their M&A strategy. This will be able to grow the company at the fastest pace and also potentially increase profits significantly. Along with maximizing the returns for mergers and acquisitions, another effective strategy for the CFO is to ensure that the company is not a victim of a hostile take-over attack. The CFO will need to remain vigilant and ensure that they can prevent any of these types of attempts which could prove deadly to an otherwise thriving company.

CHAPTER 13 – SHARE PRICE

One way to measure success for a new CFO of a publicly-traded company would be how well the stock price is doing. If a stock price rises one generally can determine that the company is doing well, while a stock that has a declining price can indicate a struggling company and hence would reflect poorly on both the CEO and CFO.

If we take an example of Company X and we say that the price of their stock has risen by 5% today alone. One would come to the conclusion that the company is earning profits and doing better than expected and hence, one would assume that both the CEO and CFO are leading well and are successful. However, what if that same stock lost 10% of its value the day before, would you come with the same conclusion? Definitely, not. If the price had not fluctuated much for the past year or so and all of a sudden, the price dropped by 10% on one day and then recovered 5% on the next day, this would overall be negative. Hence, the stock price may be one indicator but it is not the only indicator. One would not say the company was doing very poorly on the day it lost 10% and then very well on the day it gained 5%. Despite that the company had an increase in one day, the overall effect was a net decrease and all things being equal, we would need to conclude that the company is not performing as well as expected.

One final example, let us take Company Y, and they are reviewing their estimates based on strong earnings in the quarter. Now, their estimates are showing much higher growth. This new growth that is now quite a bit larger, would cause a very large increase in the valuation of the company. This would reflect well in the prices and the stocks would grow immediately. One could argue that they are doing quite well. If however, the increased gain was due to an issue that is more of a one-off situation and not likely to reoccur or cause the company to experience great growth over the next few years. Then, the increase in stock prices would be short-lived and this would be evident within the next few quarterly reports. This would cause a short term gain, then many would conclude that the company is being run very well until the expected growth is not seen and the stocks would come back to where they were or perhaps even lower. This would not be a positive result for the company, it would show stock prices that rise and fall very rapidly. All stocks can, and do vary in price, but generally, the percentages are quite low. A volatile stock may fluctuate up to 5% in a day, where most stocks do not fluctuate more than 1% in a day. In reality, it is hard to get a good idea of how well the company is being run by using stock prices over a short period. On the other hand, over many years, the stock price would be a good measure of the success or lack of success of a company. You would need to account for any effect of dividends, as these will have an effect of lowering the price of a share. However, if we take dividends out of the equation or correct the price for any dividends paid, then the price of shares may be a good indicator of the success of the company and therefore of the success of the CFO and CEO.

Increasing Prices and Performance

If the price of the shares of Company X has increased 25% over the past five years, one may conclude that this is a good increase and hence they are performing well. But, if the average company during the same period increased their share price by 45%, then they would be poorly performing, however, if this market only increased 10% during this time frame, then they would be performing much better than average. Hence, it is not as simple as if the prices increase that determines if they are performing well. You may even have a situation wherein one year the Company lost 5% of its value, one may conclude they are performing poorly, but if the environment was 2008, where many companies saw a loss of 50% of their value overnight, then this would be a very positive outcome. Therefore, you need to look at how the company is performing compared to the market that they are in to determine good performance or not. As well, one has to understand the full condition of the company before one can make a definitive conclusion. Usually, the public may not have access to this information and hence, the best way to value the performance of a company would be to compare it to its peers in the same market. What is the return on equity and what is the return on assets, these would be good indicators of success. If one looks solely at the return on assets, then those that are highly leveraged will not compete as well, but if you compare the earnings before interest and taxes (EBIT), this will allow you to compare two companies that have a similar asset base but that are very differently leveraged, one with high debt and one with low debt. It is also important to not just consider the point it is at today, but a very critical issue is the growth. Hence, if two companies are both earning the same EBIT per total assets, the formula that takes EBIT and divides it by total assets will get the basic earning power or (BEP), then they may be considered as performing equally, but if we go one year prior and see that one of those companies had a BEP of 5% less than this year, while the other had 10% less. One may feel that the consistently stronger one should be higher valued, however, the reality is growth is a far greater contributor to price than earnings and the company that earned less relatively in the year prior would have greater growth, as such, their share price would grow more. In summary, it is not just the BEP today, but it is also the growth in BEP that is a major issue, and those companies that can grow their BEP faster and more consistently will see their share prices increase the greatest, all other things being more or less equal.

Basic Earning Power

The positive thing about using BEP is that it takes away the leveraging to see how the company is performing with regards to pure assets, which is important to understand. One should also take into account the leveraging of the assets. Hence, if one company funds all of their assets with equity and no debt, while another company leverages its assets to equity with a ratio of 5 to 1. Hence, if they have $200 M in equity, they would have $1 B in assets. They would incur far more interest costs but if their assets are earning much better than the average interest cost, this could be a situation where the company performs very well. One could look at the return on equity (ROE), this would now not look at EBIT but would need to look at net profit, to be fair, then divide this by the equity. A company with a better ROE would be one that is performing very well when taking into account the leveraging.

If we compare two companies X and Y, and we compare their ROE and BEP, if company X has a higher BEP than company Y but company Y has a higher ROE than company X, then in this situation it would be difficult to determine which company one should invest in. The one with the more potential is the one with the higher BEP, but the one that is leveraging their assets better is the one with the higher ROE. If the differences in ROE are very significant then it may be best to go with the higher ROE. But, if company X can start leveraging their assets better, then company X may be the better choice.

Many Factors to Consider

Hence, the stock prices takes a lot of factors into consideration and it is not one alone that wins over the others. In the end, the stock prices over a longer period would be a good estimation of the performance of the company and therefore both the CEO and CFO. Ultimately, shareholders that see their stocks increase in value are far less likely to want to change either their CEO or CFO and this is ultimately a good indication of good performance. The one caveat is that the financial figures should be real and not over-stated if the financial figures are falsely reported, then a much better picture could be presented. This could lead to a temporary price increase, but ultimately it will fall and potentially be completely wiped out. In this situation, one might falsely rate the company as successful, and both the CEO and CFO. While in reality not only are they not successful but they may also be quite unethical and cause the collapse of the company. Had the real numbers been reported all along, the shareholders could have removed the CEO and CFO due to poor performance and brought in people that could be of benefit to the company.

In short, if we remove gains due to speculation and other short term gains, so that we are basing our stock prices on real financial data and not data that has been unethically manufactured to distort the truth when we see sustained growth in price of shares over a period greater than one year, then we can reasonably determine that the company is a success, as long as this growth is greater than the average growth of its peers. The increase in stock price will take into account and increase in BEP and any increase in ROE. Thus, we can objectively conclude, that all things being equal, a company that outperforms their market consistently for an extended period can be concluded to be a success, and therefore, that success can also be extended to both the CEO and CFO.

CHAPTER 14 - IMPORTANCE OF FORECASTING AND ANALYSIS

"We're now exploring 'forward looking KPIs'. We're pretty good at backward looking KPIs. So now we've picked a couple of our business groups and we're working closely with them on some of the important business indicators either internal or external, that can help us be more predictive in terms of where their business is headed and what some of the gaps are, and we're seeing financial results."

—DOUG VANDERSLICE, CFO OF BOSTON CHILDREN'S HOSPITAL

Being able to determine if a decision that was made was the right or wrong decision is a crucial factor in the success of a company. The faster any decision can be determined whether it was right or wrong then the success would be far better accelerated. Imagine a company that was able to make numerous major decisions on any day, but would know within a day or two which decisions were good and which decisions were poor.

This would allow the company to cease the actions of poor decisions and continue with good decisions. The ability to do this can be accomplished with good forecasting and analysis.

Assume a company is selling a product and uses three mechanisms to sell those products, each mechanism seems good, each with costs and each with a certain amount of sales that would determine the success or a break-even point. Assume that the three mechanisms are labeled mechanisms A, B, and C. If each of these mechanisms cost $1,000 per day and the profit on each sale is $10, then each would need to sell 100 units per day to be break-even. Now imagine if we had to wait one month to get the data, then we would incur costs of $30,000 per month for each of these, but let us say that only mechanism B was successful and both A and C were only selling 25 units and 50 units respectively, while B was selling 150 units.

Analysis and Feedback Loop

After one month of running these selling mechanisms. A would have cost $30,000 and given profits of $7,500 hence, running a net loss of $22,500. Mechanism C would have cost $30,000 and given profits of $15,000 hence running a net loss of $15,000, Finally, mechanism B would have also cost $30,000 and generated profits of $45,000, thus generating a profit of $15,000. Over the entire month, there would be a total cost of $90,000 and a total revenue of $67,500, thus resulting in a loss of $22,500. If however, after one day, they were able to assess the loss of these mechanisms and put the full amount into Mechanism B, they would have had a loss of $750 on the first day by running all three mechanisms, then on the next 29 days, they would be able to generate total profits of $130,500 with costs of $ 87,000, for a net profit of $43,500, if you subtract the loss on the first day, you would have a total profit for the month of $42,750.

When comparing the switching after one day, we see a total net profit of $42,750 as compared to switching after one month we see a deficit of $22,500, this is a staggering increase of $65,250 and it changes from a significant loss to a significant gain. This is why swift forecasting and reporting are critical to the success of a company. The sooner you can get data that shows that you are going in a good direction or an incorrect direction and react to that data is the more successful that your company will be. It would be great if a company never made a mistake and always chose the right option, but this is not that likely. What is possible, is to be able to get data back that is very quick and reliable then react swiftly to that data. The faster you can get the analysis back and act on that data is the more likely a company will be successful. Even if it took the company one week to change the strategy, it would still increase profits dramatically.

Projections are key for determining where you are heading for the year. By having a good projection system in place the company will be able to know if they are on track or not. This is critical at every level, it is important to know at the top level, but it is also important to be able to drill down and find out which areas are falling behind and which ones are exceeding targets. If your company has five major segments or business lines, one will likely be performing at budgeted figures, one will be slightly behind, one slightly ahead, one very behind and one significantly ahead. When you add each of these, the total will show you that you are on target, but the reality is that three are on target or better and two are falling below target. This knowledge will allow the company to further investigate why things are not working as well with those two business lines. Is it an issue that globally affects this segment or is it specific to the company? If it is a global issue, then it may be time to reduce efforts here, if it is specific to the company, then it is important to find out exactly why this segment is failing so that corrections can be made.

Focusing Efforts

Every aspect of a business can be run better, but one must focus on those areas where great improvements will have the greatest effect. By focusing on business segments that are just running at a loss or barely breaking even, then improving this will have a significant effect on the company. If only one business segment is running at a significant deficit, then by improving this situation or limiting the loss, one could have a significant impact on the overall profitability of the company. The ability to have a strong and reliable forecasting system will allow one to identify problems very early on without having to wait until the year is finished and before it is too late. By addressing business segments that are failing on a timely basis, this would be a great advantage to ensure the overall viability of the company. Being able to just minimize a deficit so that it is not significant will result in very positive changes with very little time.

The forecasting system should be able to calculate slight changes very swiftly and ideally should be prepared daily or weekly so that any losses can be minimized. One would have to look at the differences in costs between preparing the forecasts once a month, once a week, or once a day. At the bare minimum, the forecasts should be prepared each month and where the changes can be significant the reports should be prepared weekly and even daily. If running these reports every day would result in an extra charge of $1,000 per day, but it could potentially save millions of dollars, then it is a good deal to issue them daily. If the likely savings would only amount to $10,000 then it would make better sense to run them every month. Hence, no two situations are the same, but for very large companies where there are lots of potential gains or losses, then having it run daily would make good sense. It is also important to take into account that the more frequent you run these reports the accuracy will drop to a certain level. For this reason, it is often the case that a weekly report is sufficient. Having a weekly report would cost significantly less, it would be far better than only having a monthly report. The weekly report would also be more accurate than a daily report.

The longer gap between reports allows the accuracy to go up, this is one of the issues with daily reports. You can put more money into a daily report to get it more accurate, but there is a certain cost benefit there that must be taken into account. With this in mind, for smaller organizations, a monthly report makes the best sense, for middle size companies a weekly report makes sense, with some specific reports for daily reporting, while a very large company a daily report makes good sense.

Timely Feedback

The feedback mechanism is key to operate at high efficiency. It is critical to know when you are making changes that those changes are having a positive effect or a negative effect. This feedback mechanism should be timely, accurate, and cost-effective. The time to know when to put more resources to have a quicker turn-around time for reporting is when the costs to get the reports in a more timely manner are less than the likely benefits from knowing the information more quickly. Hence, if it costs an additional $500,000 to go from weekly reports to daily reports, but the average savings per day would be approximately 10% or an expected savings of $50,000 per day, then it is clear that one should go with the higher frequency reporting. The benefits would be calculated at $50,000 times 10% or $5,000 per day, over 365 days, this is greater than the annual cost of $500,000. If on the other hand, the benefits are only 10% of an expected savings of $5,000 per day, then, in this case, the likely benefits would not be higher than the increased cost and it would not be wise to go with the daily reporting versus the weekly reporting. The calculation would be $5,000 times 10% or $500 per day and multiplied by 365, which is less than $500,000 for the annual costs. This is why the larger the company, the more likely it is that daily reporting is warranted as opposed to weekly reporting.

It is important to make a distinction between complex financial data and simple financial data. Data such as daily sales volume are quite simple and all systems will be able to prepare this daily without a significant increase in costs. Hence, all should have these reports daily and perhaps even hourly, if need be. For those reports that are more complex, such as preparing full financial statements and projections versus actual, these reports are more complex and these reports are the type of reports that can be done monthly, weekly or daily, depending on the size of the company and the cost-benefit analysis of each.

CHAPTER 15 - BUSINESS SEGMENT

"If you save a dollar, you'll drop a dollar to the bottom line. But if you save a dollar and you reinvest that back into the business in a disciplined way, a returns-based way, that dollar is actually worth a lot more in the future. And that's really what running a business is all about."

— CATHIE LESJAK, CFO OF HP

A business segment within a company would be defined as a subsection of the overall business as a whole. These business segments can be divisible by distinct activities, distinct revenues and expenses, and potentially a distinct business model. The business segment must be divisible from other aspects of the business. One can think of the entire business as a collection of separate business segments, where the sum of all the segments is equal to the sum of the whole.

Segments of the Business

Dividing a company into business segments is a critical function to be able to see which segments are earning profits and which segments are incurring losses. The CFO must be able to generate reports that can properly divide the revenues and expenses to their proper segment. If the current reporting does not allow for this, this must be corrected immediately. This should also be done for the balance sheet, that way the company can see how much revenue is being generated per dollar of assets.

If you are a company that produces both shorts and long pants, and you can see that the overall company is running at a small profit but are not able to see the different segments separately, then you will be very hard-pressed (no pun intended) to make the correct decisions about how to improve or to correct a situation. If we imagine a company X that has an overall $ 1 M in profits and it has two segments A and B, but we are not able to break down the revenues and expenses between these two segments. We will not be able to determine which segment we should increase and which one we should decrease or potentially close down.

If we are later able to breakdown the numbers further and we see that segment A makes $ 5 M profit per year but segment B incurs a deficit of $4 M per year. Then we would have many options available to us, once this information is available. We could take resources away from segment B and direct them to segment A, thus increasing the overall profits of segment A while reducing the losses in segment B. We could also decide to close down fully the operations of segment B and put those resources to segment A, thus maximizing the profits of the company.

Usually, things are not so cut and dry, there would be many more factors to take into account, for example, segment B may be in the start-up phase and this level of loss was expected. However, if both started at the same time and both were expected to have an equal return then it would be far more likely that a correction needs to take place. The correction would require a reduction in resources for segment B or removal of segment B from the business. It is critical to first get a full understanding of why segment

B has underperformed so dramatically and see if there are potential ways to correct, without having to reduce or eliminate this segment.

Available Financial Analysis to Assess Segments

The CFO would play a crucial role in ensuring that the data is available to be able to compare multiple segments with each other. The CFO and their teams would need to investigate any segments that are underperforming to understand why they are underperforming and what corrections can be made to alleviate this situation.

Along with the CEO, the CFO and other executives would decide how much resources to allocate for each segment. Along with the business leaders of each segment, budgets and forecasts would be prepared and agreed to by each segment leader. Then once the results came in, the segment leaders would need to explain why they are either performing well or are under-performing. It would be critical that the CFO would prepare reports where both the CEO and CFO would be able to quickly look at some KPIs for each segment and see how they are doing. Are they meeting their revenue targets? Are their costs under control? Is the profit or loss projection on track? By having a series of "traffic signals" or something similar, one can quickly see which is at the green, yellow, or red. The red would require immediate attention, the green would signify they are on target or doing better. While the yellow would signify that they are slightly behind the target. The CFO and CEO would need to decide when this needs to be addressed. If it is a small issue, it would be fine to have a quick discussion about the issue and see what happens next month. Then the next month they would to verify if the situation resolved itself or is it getting worse?

CHAPTER 16 - INVESTMENT BASICS

Business valuation is a key component of investing. When you can estimate the true value of a company, you can then calculate its ideal stock price and determine whether a company is overvalued or undervalued. As well, if you are considering acquiring or a merger, it is critical to be able to value the business both before and after a merger.

Business Valuation

To get a strong estimate of the value of a company, you must be able to reasonably estimate what are the likely profits for the next thirty to forty years. Then you would take the net present value of those future revenue streams to estimate the value of the company. You must have a good idea of what the growth rates will be and how risky are these revenue streams. You must decide on a discount rate to be used for these calculations and you must ensure that the expected growth rate is included in your formulas.

Hence, if you have a company that is currently earning $1 M per year and is expected to earn the same amount over the next forty years, assuming a discount rate of 5%, this company would have a net present value (NPV) of approximately $17 M. If one million shares are outstanding, this would yield a stock price of $17 per share. It would have a P/E ratio of 17. This would fall into a reasonable range for P/E ratios. For the purposes of this calculation, we did not factor in a growth rate. But, most companies should be expected to grow at least at the rate of inflation.

If that same company still had the same discount rate but was now expected to grow by 10% each year, the calculations would be very different. The NPV would now be $108 M, and its stock price would now be $108 per share and have a P/E ratio of 108. This illustrates the effect of growth rates on the valuation of a company.

To exaggerate this point even further, if the company was expected to grow at 20% per year over the next forty years, it would now have an NPV of $1.385 B. Its share price would be $1,385 per share and have a P/E ratio of 1,385. Such a growth rate for such an extended period of time, is not that reasonable, but if it was reasonable, that would be the valuation.

Growth Estimates

Estimating the growth rate and estimating the discount rate to use are major factors that would affect the valuation of a company. When you now have this business valuation, you can decide whether to invest in a company or not. By understanding the value of a company, you can determine whether a company is overvalued or undervalued

Investment in Machinery

A company will often need to determine whether they should purchase a piece of machinery or not. This can also be determined from an NPV calculation or a cost-benefit analysis.

If we know that a machine will cost us $ 1 M today, but we expect that machine to reduce our costs of production by 20% over the next 20 years, if we assume that our cost of borrowing is 5% and we assume that our costs of production are about $0.8 M with an expected growth rate of 3%. We can estimate the NPV of the future benefits to achieve a value of $2.6 M. This would mean that the benefits far exceed the costs and that the machine is a very good investment. The NPV of future savings will be far greater than the investment cost. One must also take into account qualitative factors, but with such a high NPV, it would be hard to override the quantitative analysis.

The calculation of the net present value is critical when looking at business valuations and determining whether it makes sense to purchase a piece of machinery or not.

Expanding into a new Business Segment

When considering whether to invest in developing a new business segment, preparing a cost-benefit analysis is critical. At the heart of the cost-benefit analysis will be estimating the net present value of various costs and the net present value of revenues. This will determine whether it is wise to build up a new business segment or not. There are many qualitative factors to also consider such as, does it enhance your brand or take away from your brand. These qualitative factors could play a more important factor than the quantitative analysis. If we are to assume there are no major issues on the qualitative side and we can see that the initial investment will be $1 M for the first three years and during that period there will be no revenues, but after that, there will be $500 K of revenues and growing at a 10% rate. When we look at the NPV of the costs we get a value of $2.72 M, while when we look at the revenues for the next ten years we see a value of $3.85 M. Since the NPV of the revenues are greater than the NPV of the investment it is a good deal. The overall NPV of this business would be $1.13 M. Also, this business would continue to grow beyond the next ten years, hence, it would even have a larger NPV.

Internal Rate of Return

Another way to value these decisions is by calculating the internal rate of return (IRR), this would be the rate of return where the costs and revenues are equal. If we look at the example of the machinery that costs $1 M but saves us $160 K per year but this grows at 3% per year, this would have an IRR of 12%. The higher the IRR the better. If your discount rate is 6%, then since the IRR is greater than your discount rate this would mean that this is a great investment. The rate that you decide an investment is good or not is called the hurdle rate. In this case, the hurdle rate was set at 6%, since the IRR is 12%, which is higher than the hurdle, the conclusion is that this is a good investment.The advantage of using IRR is that it can compare projects of unequal size. For example, if we are looking at two potential investments in machinery and one costs $2 M, but the other costs $ 5 M. It may very well be that the investment of $5 M yields a higher NPV than the investment of $2 M, but if the IRR of the $2 M is higher than that of the $5 M investment, there is a good argument to proceed with the higher IRR investment. Since the additional funds could be used to fund similarly higher IRR projects.

Knowing your borrowing rate and your discount rate is essential to calculate any NPV. You may decide that your discount rate is equal to your borrowing rate or you may have a justification for an increased rate or a lowered rate. The calculation of an IRR does not require to have the discount rate in the formula, it is simply compared to the discount rate or your hurdle rate. If the IRR is greater than the discount rate then the investment is good. The higher the IRR the better the investment is. There are times where the discount rate is not valid or even negative, this would be where the future revenue streams would never equal the investment cost. Hence, if you have a $ 1 M investment and for the next 10 years it results in savings of $50 K, the total of those future revenue streams is less than the $1 M cost and hence will require a negative value, which does not exist, logically. If the savings was $100 K per year the value of the IRR would be zero. This IRR is going to be lower than most hurdle rates or discount rates and as such would not be a good investment. If however, it would save $200 K per year it would have an IRR of 15%. This is a very strong IRR and would be higher than most hurdle rates. The hurdle rate is the IRR rate where the investment is deemed positive. Hence, if your hurdle rate is 8% and your IRR is 15%, then the investment exceeds the hurdle rate and hence it is a good investment.

The IRR calculation is great to rank different investment options and allow one to choose the one with the highest profitability potential, even where investments are of different sizes.

CHAPTER 17 – COST BENEFIT ANALYSIS

– PRAVIN SHAH

Another critical tool used by most CFOs would be the preparation and review of a cost-benefit analysis. This analysis is critical whenever you are looking to make an investment decision. Any significant investment should go through a cost-benefit analysis before proceeding. This way one can get a good understanding of whether the investment is worthwhile or not.

For example, let us say that you are looking to invest $ 5 M in creating a solar farm. You would need to look at the cost side, let's assume for simplicity that the cost is simply the cost of the solar panels and their installation which would cost $ 5 M. The next step would be to look at the cost savings over the next ten or twenty years. If you are to assume that giving the amount of energy you can save will amount to about $ 500 K per year, as well, this is likely to grow by about 3% due to expected increases in electricity costs. You can now estimate the net present value (NPV) of these future savings by using the following formula.

NPV = Savings times IRR over 20 years which gives a value of $ 6.5 M, the actual calculation is a lot more complex it would be the summation of each of the net present values for each of the 20 years to today's date, any year X can be estimated by the following formula $500 K multiplied by (1 + 0.03) to the power of X, then divided by (1 + DR) to the power of X. Luckily, calculators, tables, and computers can make these calculations much easier for you.

Internal Rate of Return for Decision Making
As well, you could impute the IRR of this investment. If the IRR is greater than your cost of borrowing or your hurdle rate, then this is likely a good investment.

If the NPV exceeds $ 5 M, which in this case amounts to $ 6.5 M, this indicates that this investment is a very good investment and yields a positive NPV. One would also need to evaluate the qualitative factors that go into this analysis and after reviewing both the quantitative and qualitative analysis a conclusion and recommendation can be made. If we are to assume that the qualitative analysis also indicates that there are more benefits than costs, then the recommendation would be to proceed with the investment. Hence, the idea to invest in a solar farm would proceed ahead, should there be existing funds to invest.

Putting the cost-benefit analysis on a spreadsheet is a must, as the formulas can be quite complex but in a spreadsheet, they can be made quite easily.

When funds are limited and there exist several different projects that can be invested in. One can impute the internal rate of return

(IRR), this is the rate of return where the costs equal the NPV of future revenue streams. The higher the IRR the more positive will be the net present value in relative terms, compared with lower IRR investments. The positive thing about calculating the IRR for various projects is that they can be compared to the IRR and the ones with the highest IRRs can be chosen. This way if you have three or four investment possibilities you can rate them in order by the IRR. The IRR also takes into account the size of the investment. Hence, one investment may have a larger net present value but could have a lower IRR. To make the most profit, the ones with the highest IRRs should be chosen first. This assumes that qualitative analysis is very much the same. There are times where the qualitative analysis may override the quantitative analysis. This could be the case if there are some potential reputational risks with a given investment or other risks that deem the investment not warranted to undertake at the moment.

Significant Decisions

With every significant decision that is made through a cost-benefit analysis, it is important to track whether the forecasts of future revenues are being met or not. This is important to be able to improve your forecasting and also to justify the decisions that were made. Should an investment decision end up being a poor decision, by having this analysis one will be able to review what went wrong with the analysis. Were the future revenues estimates too optimistic? Were there certain costs that were not taken into account? Or was there a significant change in the environment that was outside of your control which had a negative effect? All potential reasons for a variance should be looked at, this will improve your estimates going forward.

CHAPTER 18 – WHY A SUCCESSFUL CFO IS NECESSARY

"We see opportunity to continue to grow revenue in excess of audience in the near term as we continue to improve ad formats and drive better relevance and deliver a better ROI ultimately for advertisers. But ultimately, growing the base of people who use the platform is the lifeblood of the company and that's going to be our focus as we continue to invest and drive growth in the next few years."

— NED SEGAL, CFO OF TWITTER

The function of a CFO in a company is a critical function and one that cannot be replaced. The success of a company can be strongly linked between the CEO and CFO. It is important to understand that most CEOs cannot perform the functions of a CFO. For the most part, they do not have the required skills or experience, as well, they certainly do not have the time to perform these functions. There are some CEOs that were previously the CFO of the company. In this case, this CEO should ensure that they do not continue acting as the CFO, this would not work well for the company, nor for the CEO or the CFO.

CFOs that Became CEO

The one exception to this general rule, are those CEOs that started as a CFO, in this case, they have the abilities but will not have the time to perform these roles. The CFO is necessary for the company to be highly profitable and highly efficient. This role with the successful CFO will have a positive effect with external parties and with internal partners. This role plays an overall vital role in the success of the company.

The CEO also plays a critical role and the most critical role in the success of a company, however, the CEO alone cannot perform all the functions of a successful CFO. Hence, the CFO role is equally required for the success of a company. In some ways, the CFO role can be seen as fulfilling two major functions, the first one is providing all the necessary analysis and judgment for the CEO to lead the company to success and maximizing profitability. The other additional role is that if the CEO is performing improperly or poorly, they are a safeguard for this situation. This is particularly true where the reporting line of the CFO is not direct to the CEO but rather to the Board. This has the added benefit of acting as a safeguard for a weak CEO. You can imagine a parachute, the CEO would be the primary chute, but if this fails then you would need the secondary to fill in the function. Without this there could be severe consequences, the same is true if you have a weak CEO and a situation where the CFO reports directly to that CEO. In this case, you only would have one primary chute and if this fails, a lot of damage will be done before it is possible to correct the situation.

Providing Leadership

The CFO provides great leadership, they ensure their teams run smoothly, and provides reports to all other teams so that each team can make the best and quickest possible decisions to improve their profitability, efficiency, and overall operations. The CFO also provides insight to the CEO and plays a major role in the overall strategy and direction of the company. It will be next to impossible to find a company that is very successful and it does not contain both a successful CEO and a successful CFO. The CEO and CFO must both understand that concept, for the company to be successful, both of them must be successful and their relationship must flourish.

Mismatch

It is possible to have one of the two roles be successful and the other role to be struggling, but this would result in a moderately successful company at best and only for a limited time. If the CEO is performing above expectations and the CFO is performing below expectations, it should be a rather short period before the CEO realizes this situation and correct this issue. This situation, with a decent CEO, should not last more than a few months. They would quickly realize that the recommendations coming from the CFO are lacking or some part of their job is lacking. This would not have a major impact on operations, as it would not last long. In the situation of a weak CEO and a strong CFO, this situation is more complex. If the CEO decides to listen to the CFO, then the company can flourish despite having a weak CEO. In essence, the CFO would be running the company. This can work for an indefinite period. The problem here is that there may be some resentment building up between the two, in this situation. Both would quickly understand who the real leader is and who is making the decisions. If both can live with this situation, it can last for years. Often, in this situation, the CEO starts to feel threatened by the CFO and starts to make their own decisions, against the advice of the CFO. This can start to lead to a disaster. The CEO then has two options, he can begin listening to the advice of the CFO again or dig his heels in further, the latter would have a significant and negative effect on the company.

From the above it is clear that the most ideal situation is where both the CEO and CFO are strong, the second-best situation is where the CEO is strong and the CFO is weak. The situation where the CFO is strong and the CEO is weak but listens to the CFO is also a net positive outcome, but the situation where the CEO is weak and does not listen to the CFO is the worst of all situations. While this situation is very negative, it is less negative, if the CFO does not report directly to the CEO.

Looking at the analysis it is clear that both the CEO and CFO play a critical role in the success of the company and it is somewhat arguable which plays a greater role, both are critically important and the success of the company depends on the success of both roles. The role of the CEO, in the end, may be very slightly more critical than the CFO. Most highly successful CEOs would also need to have a highly successful CFO. As well, when the CEO is strong and paired with a weak CFO, this can easily be fixed by the CEO. On the other hand, if a strong CFO is paired with a weak CEO, it is not so easy for the CFO to fix this situation, as a result, the CEO role is more important than the CFO.

To illustrate the importance of both of these roles, one can see that both are required to sign and certify for financial information, this would be true for the annual audited financial statements and as well, for any financial information provided to the Securities Exchange Commission (SEC). Both can be held personally liable for any misconstruction of information to some degree.

Sarbanes-Oxley

This new requirement came as one of the new rules under Sarbanes-Oxley after the crash of both Enron and WorldCom roughly twenty years ago. In both of those cases, the CEO argued that they were unaware of what was going on with the financial accounting of the business that they were running. For this to be true, one would have to envisage a situation where the CFO wanted to take control of the company and duped the CEO by giving them information that was either false or not understandable. The reality is that no one believed that this could be true as it is very far fetched. A CEO who argues that they do not understand financial accounting would be one that states I was not competent to do my job so I should not be held responsible for the mess that got us to this point. It is for this lack of a convincing argument that Sarbanes-Oxley requires both the CEO and CFO to sign the financial data and attest to their fairness.

It would be interesting to see how much overlap did the CEO have in the roles of the CFOs in these two cases. In similar situations, one can imagine that the CFO and CEO worked very closely together. The CFO would likely keep the CEO very much in the loop. A strong CEO would understand that something is amiss with the company and would not be very likely to believe a rosy picture presented to them by the CFO. It is also important to understand that both the CEO and the CFO would benefit from such an environment rather than the CFO alone. As the CFO reports in some way to the CEO, it would be likely that the CFO would inform the CEO, but if this were something that was not legal, it is very likely that it would not be done through email or in any written documents.

Supervisory Role
In most cases where one position controls the other, it is far more likely that the CEO controls the CFO, probably about 99% of the cases, where one is controlled by the other. Fortunately, in a well-governed company, the CFO does not report directly to the CEO and this controlling of the CFO is still a risk but it is far less risky.

Auditor Role
The auditors also played a very large role in the downfall of these companies and a reason why the big-six is now referred to as the big-four. Another strong reason to have a reliable CFO is to avoid these types of situations, there should also be a separate commit-

tee to look at the balance sheet and see that all makes good sense. If one sees some unusual accounting treatments, this should be explained by both the CFO and CEO. Especially if there is a big change in accounting treatment that has a material effect on the financial statements.

Ethics and Integrity

A good CFO will also have a high degree of ethics and these ethics can be the difference from a company that is doomed to failure and one that comes clean about their situation and then the problem is looked after and resolved. If a company is going through very tough times, the CFO must be very upfront with the Board, with the shareholders, and with the public, if they intentionally try to hide the problem, they will make things worse and this action could cause the whole collapse of the company. The CFO and CEO must be both individuals with a high degree of honesty, integrity, and ethics. If either or both are not ethically sound, this would present major challenges for the company. If one demonstrates a lack of character or ethics, it is better to find someone that does possess those traits. If more ethics were on display before the utter collapse at some of these companies, perhaps the bankruptcy could have been avoided.

A strong CFO is required to give the company the proper direction, to ensure the best decisions are being made, to provide others with financial analysis to make the most informed decisions, and to provide a counter-balance should the CEO not be on the right track. Both the CEO and the CFO should possess the highest degree of integrity and ethics, if either of them is weak in this area, it would be time to look for their replacement - sooner than later.

CHAPTER 19 - RISK APPETITE OF THE CFO

*"In this era of 'free money,' it's still critical to remember cash gener-
ation — or, rather, consistent and material cash generation. It's the
biggest factor in the long-term success of any business. This might
sound textbook, but that's because it's true. Revenue growth and
disciplined expense management will generate the cash a business
needs to invest, seize growth opportunities, and return consistent
value to owners."*

— JOHN STEPHENS, THE CFO OF AT&T

This might sound textbook, but that's because it's true. Revenue growth and disciplined expense management will generate the cash a business needs to invest, seize growth opportunities, and return consistent value to owners."

We have all heard expressions like where there is no risk there is no reward. To some extent this is true but there is something that we can call good risk, there is a mitigated risk and there is a bad risk.

The successful CFO will know when to take on more risk and

when that risk is acceptable and when it is not. One area that can be significant is the amount of leverage that the company should have. By taking out more debt, you are taking on more risk. The debt comes with a fixed interest rate whether you make a profit or do not. While taking on more equity does not require a fixed payment. Hence, the debt is higher risk, but this higher risk can be beneficial to the shareholders of a company. There are two main ratios that we should look at in financial analysis when looking at leverage. The first one is the debt ratio, this one is simply the total debt divided by the total assets. Hence, if a company has $50 M of debt and $100 M of assets, this would have a debt ratio of 0.5 or 50%. One could say that this is high or this is low, depends on the situation and the market as a whole.

Debt to Equity Ratio
The next important ratio is the debt-to-equity ratio, this is defined as the total debt divided by the total equity. In this example, the debt would be $50 M and the equity is also $50 M, hence this ratio would be 1.0 or 100%. If the debt was $100 M and equity was $20 M, the ratio would be 5.0 or 500%.

There are some advantages to having a lower debt to equity ratio, the first advantage would be that it is a safer environment. If business hits a low period, there would not be a significant sum to pay in interest and capital. As well, those companies with a low debt to equity ratio would be in a better position to take on new debt, and hence, they would have the advantage to grow. The advantages of companies with a high debt to equity ratio would most likely come in the form of a strong return on equity. If two companies could both earn 10% profits on assets, but one is highly leveraged and the other is not, then the highly leveraged company would earn a higher ROE than the less leveraged company, with the assumption that the interest rate being paid is reasonable and far less than 10%. Hence, leveraging the company can be maximizing profits for the company and its shareholders. Although usually after significantly increasing your leverage, you would need to invest those funds, hence, a heavily leveraged company would have recently had an expansion or growth in their business. This should reflect what has occurred with the company in the past year or two. After some time, the debt should be able to be paid off and with the extra earnings, there would also be additional retained earnings which is also equity. As a result, the debt to equity ratio would drop. If not dropping, this could indicate that the company is having some difficulties in being profitable or paying the interest burden. Another item to look out for is whether the company is paying a significant portion of net income as dividends. This fact would keep the debt to equity ratio higher, than if no dividends were paid. Losses would also make the debt to equity ratio higher and that much riskier.

How much Risk is too much?
It is imperative that the CFO understands how much risk can be taken on and how much risk is too much when considering how much debt the company can increase by. If they are already at a risky level, they should consider measures to reduce their debt rather than increase it. By getting an optimal debt to equity ratio, the CFO can ensure the best ROE for the company without exposing the company to too much risk.

The risk of a given merger or acquisition is important for all facets to be taken into account, but most of all, the overall business risk. Will this merger work, will the merger add value, and will each individual companies culture work together? These are all important factors to take into account. If a merger could potentially cost the company many of its clients due to reputation issues of the merging company. This should be assessed prior to any merger. Are the corporate beliefs and cultures compatible, if not, this could pose a lot of issues? A merger or an acquisition has a high degree of risk and the right company should be chosen to acquire or merge with. In addition to this critical issue, the CFO must be able to determine when this approach is the right approach. It may be not the right time to merge and not the right time to acquire. Perhaps there is a less risky way to achieve growth or a less risky way to achieve that same objective that one is expecting to achieve through the merger or acquisition. On the other hand, it may be the best decision and the least risky decision to move forward. This understanding of risk and reward with regards to mergers and acquisitions is critical for the CFO to understand in order for the CFO to be successful with M&A. The successful approach here could be the one area that generates the most growth of a company and if done incorrectly it could be the one thing that sets back a company many years and even potentially ruins the company. One just needs to think of a couple of disastrous mergers in our recent history, such as the AOL Time Warner merger.

Avoiding Potentially Disastrous Mergers

Strong CFOs will allow companies to avoid such disastrous decisions. However, if the CEO wants to move forward on one, at least a CFO can recommend a different approach. With great risk can come great reward, but if one is risking the entire company then this is not a risk that is worth taking. If a merger does not add value to both companies then it should not be undertaken.

The CFO must understand the risks that the company is facing and when it is a good time to take on additional risk, as well, when it is the right time to lower your risk. It is ideal that by maintaining a manageable level of risk, that one can ensure good growth and increase profitability, but by taking on too much risk, you run the risk of reducing all the progress you made and even run the risk of ruining the company. There is a time to mitigate or reduce your risk and there is a time to take on additional risk and additional challenges. This is critical for a company to take advantage and grow quickly but not to leave themselves too leveraged and too exposed. Balancing the right amount of risk to add or reduce is a key factor for the success of the company, with too little risk there will not be as much growth and with too much risk, the whole company could pay a steep price, if things fail.

CHAPTER 20 – INTERNAL AND EXTERNAL FACTORS

For a CFO to be successful, they must have certain attributes. Without possession of these internal attributes, it will be difficult to succeed no matter what the external factors are. Hence, even with the best company in the world, having an incapable CFO may turn that into a failing position. While on the other hand, the most competent CFO may be able to turn a very weak company into a thriving company over some years. If the company has no strength and the best way forward is for the company to close down, the competent CFO will also be able to make this determination and thus save the shareholders and investors from wasting further resources, although generally as eternal optimists they will look t find a possible solution and may just find one.

Ethics

The successful CFO must have a high degree of ethics. If the ethics of the CFO are not at the highest level, then this will play a factor in all teams under him and all teams that he works with. The CFO, even more than the CEO, should be the standard-setter for ethics within the company. The CEO, also, should have a very high degree of integrity and ethics. This is a very critical area, if the CFO is known to not put up with unethical people or situations, then that will send a message across his teams and the company. This is beneficial for all, the company, the CEO, the CFO, the shareholders, the partners, and all investors. This is a critical strength for the CFO.

Business Analysis

Another critical strength is the ability to understand the business and come up with the best solutions. They should be a strong "numbers guy" but also much more than just that. The successful CFO must understand where the business is heading and which areas can help grow profits and grow the business. This will aid in ensuring the best solutions are chosen. If the CFO does not possess an abundance of strength here, then at best they can be a mediocre CFO. One needs to be able to come up with the right solutions and ensure they are selected.

Leadership

Along with having great business analysis capabilities, the successful CFO must be a strong leader. It is not enough to come up with the right solutions. You must be able to convince others that your solutions are correct, otherwise, they will not be implemented. In that case, it would not matter if you came up with the right or wrong decision if that decision is not implemented. This is a critical strength to have and generally an area where most CFOs already have, to get to that role, however, it is important to still note this as a necessary strength.

Results-Oriented

Connected with leadership, one must ensure that solutions are implemented. Hence, being able to convince others that you have the right solution requires leadership, but then one must possess the right managerial skills to ensure the solutions are implemented and then ensure that the expected results are achieved. It is very hard to argue that a person without results is a good leader and conversely, it is hard to argue that a person that drives results is not a good leader. In short, to drive results, you must come up with a good solution, you must then convince others to implement the decision, then you must oversee the implementation of the solution, to some extent, when all of these are done, then one may achieve results. When many people are asked what is necessary to have for a good leader, the best and most consistent answer is always, results.

Team Building

Another skill that we discussed is the ability to motivate teams, create teams, lead teams, and manage teams to great results that are necessary for the successful CFO. The CFO is only as strong as the teams he has developed, the systems they created, and the partnerships they have nurtured. A CFO is one person and there is no way that this person can achieve everything alone, they must create a strong team and must delegate tasks effectively to individuals that can deliver. They must find ways to delegate and motivate teams and individuals. Without this ability, the CFO will struggle and the company will struggle as well.

These are some of the most critical internal factors that a CFO must possess to ensure the success of a company. We can look at the success of a company and then infer that due to that success both the CEO and CFO are successful. This would be correct most of the time. But it does not tell the full story and in fact, this may be quite misleading in reality.

If we look at company A, and it has everything going for it, the company is earning strong profits, has a very powerful BEP ratio with a strong ROE, then this company is running very well. In this case, a CFO that holds up the fort and ensures that very little changes are made can be viewed as quite successful. However, to ensure things run as they are currently running is far more simple than requiring a complete overhaul of operations. It may be that even a mediocre CFO could ensure that things are running as they were running. In this case, a mediocre CFO would be rated as the company is rated and thus be estimated as being very strong. This CFO may not require all the strengths of a strong CFO to maintain success. If this CFO is told that they are not to rock the boat, the expectation is that they keep running the company as was run for the past ten or twenty years. Then they will be performing that minimal task and will be rated highly, but it will be very difficult to assess if they are capable of being far more successful, as they are told, to just keep things running as they are.

On the other hand, if you have another company, company B, where they are very much struggling and currently have a low BEP ratio, a negative ROE and are facing several years of deficits. Then a CFO taking over the reins of this company would be at a significant disadvantage compared to a new CFO of company A. If after one year, the company reports another loss, the CFO may be rated as a failure since the company remains failing. If however, the company has improved its financial position significantly, the CFO may be a huge success. Hence, it is not always easy just to look at results and make the conclusion that the CFO is successful or the CFO is not successful. Although without knowing the day to day activities of the CFO, then this is the only information that is available to rate their performance.

Measuring Success

A better measurement of success would be the trend of the business. If a new CFO can reduce deficits or increase profits, then they can be viewed as more successful. This is a better tool to determine success. However, one must also recognize that in many situations trends are also inherited from the previous CFO or exist before a new CFO joins. Hence, one would need to evaluate the change of the trend. Let us say that a company is growing at 3% per year and expected to grow at 3%, that would be the trend. If now the trend is lowered to 2%, then this could indicate a poor performance from the CFO and CEO. If however, the company is now growing at 4%, then the CFO has improved this trend and hence, they can be viewed as more successful. These changes in trends will also reflect a change in stock prices, much greater than would occur without a change in the trend.

An analogy to this would be having a coach and a team. If we take a hockey coach and a hockey team, you may have the best hockey coach in the world, but if they are coaching a team with no talent and little experience, it will be almost impossible for that team to beat a team that has excessive talent, even if that team has a very weak coach. You could have a very weak coach, and coach a team like Team Canada in hockey and they will do very well and even very likely win. While on the other hand, you could have the best hockey coach in the world coach a poorly performing team and they will still likely lose. The coach can make a difference but there are also other necessary factors for success apart from the coach.

Just like the coaching example, the best and most qualified CFOs can only accomplish so much when they are running a company that has many inherent challenges. If a company is loaded with debt and does not have any profits coming in, this company will be very difficult to turn around, but given time the CFO will be able to take steps to improve matters, but it may take five or six years before results begin to show. Similarly, a weak CFO that takes over a very strong company will continue to make very strong results for many years but over time, the company will become less competitive, and then it will be evident that there is a slow down in results. This will become clear and at this point, then it will be time to find a new CEO and CFO.

Missing a Key Component

Some companies have all the basic ingredients for success but might be lacking one. This is where bringing in a very capable CFO will improve the situation very rapidly and ensure the company can reach its potential. If a company is performing very well, but it is not very well leveraged, then the CFO can make some changes and improve results quickly. Perhaps the company is not taking advantage of any leveraging. This would negatively affect its growth potential. A new CFO would recognize this weakness and correct it, the company would be far more successful and in a relatively short period. The success of the company could grow significantly within a year or two. Hence, there are some situations where bringing the right person in will have a huge and positive effect. This would be where the companies are generally strong for the most part but are not strong on every issue.

Company Basics

If the basics of a company do not add up, or in other words, nothing works for the company, then the successful CFO will have little effect on this company for many years until they can start changing each weakness into a strength. It will remain a question whether it is better to just start over if this is the case, then the company should think about shutting down, but this would be only for those companies where they are already in serious trouble. In these situations, it has very little effect if the CFO is the most qualified or poorly qualified, the results will be poor. However, the strong CFO will be able to make improvements, these improvements will take time to show. There are certain situations that no CFO can fix or the costs to fix would be greater than the value of the company.

In a very well-performing company, where everything is working in optimal conditions, then, in this case, the strong CFO will be able to maintain this and perhaps improve it a little but it will be very hard to get a large improvement from a company that is already performing so well. At the same time, a poorly performing CFO will likely be able to maintain a lot of the trends by just keeping things moving in the same direction. It will take a few years for a less capable CFO to take a toll on a very successful company, but over time it will occur. The CFO will not adapt when the environment changes and the company will pay a hefty price. The CFO will not plan for any potential risks that are coming and the company will see a decline in results. This could happen relatively quickly, within two to three years or it may take longer, perhaps five to ten years. It will happen, but it will take some time. Hence, even a company that is very successful needs to have a strong CFO at its helm. It may be fine for a year or two, but not much longer than that, if the CFO is not very capable. Two big safeguards against a poorly performing CFO are the Board and the CEO.

In summary, the successful CFO will have a positive effect on the company that they are at the helm of, but for some, the effects may be very quick and very significant while for others this effect may take longer. On the other hand, having an incapable CFO will harm the company.

CHAPTER 21 – SMALL AND START-UP COMPANIES

Not every company can afford to pay for a strong and dedicated CFO. The starting salary would be over $150 K per year and well beyond. Many companies are struggling to make any profit at all and many are struggling to make even $ 25 K per year and more. In these situations, it would not be cost-effective to hire a CFO and create a large deficit each year. In fact, in most cases, this would be counter-productive and likely lead to failure before the company can get off its feet.

Smaller Companies

Hence for small companies and companies just starting, the functions of the CFO are usually handled by the owner. This makes good sense until the profits start to get beyond a certain point. There comes a time when the owner who is managing the company and also acting as CFO for the company can no longer do both. It may even be the case, that by having the owner try to do both, they are losing much more than the costs of having the owner focus on driving the business and handing off the responsibilities of the finances to a strong CFO.

Imagine a situation where a company now is quite profitable and earning about $500 K in profits per year. The owner who runs the company acts as both the CEO and CFO, it may be that the company can stay at that level because the manager does not have enough time to focus on growth. Now imagine, if that same company were to invest in a CFO and the cost would be approximately $150 K per year, but now the manager can grow the business at 20% per year. Within a few years the company will now be profiting $1 M or more and after paying the CFO, let us assume that the salary has grown to $200 K, would now have a net profit of $800 K and earn significantly more than the $500 K, without any growth. As well, the CEO is now getting the expert advice from the CFO and would potentially be able to increase profits by another 20% per year. Hence, potentially growing not to $ 1 M but $ 2 M. It will also reduce the amount of time required for the CEO to learn about taxes and to learn about financial reporting requirements, and external audits. This would allow the CEO to focus on what they do best and that is growing the business.

Hence, when a company is earning profits below $50 K per year it is clear that the company is not yet financially strong enough to sustain a full-time CFO then the owner should perform this function as best as they can. They can also get some assistance if they have a bookkeeper on hand or know of an accountant that they can ask for advice from time to time.

On the other hand, when a company is earning more than $500 K profits per year, then it would make sense to hire a full-time controller or CFO to take on these responsibilities and allow the owner to focus on growing the business further.

Solutions for Smaller Companies
The question is what should those companies that are growing above $50 K profit per year but not yet large enough to be able to afford a full-time CFO. There are not many options out there at this point. Most of the ones closer to $50 K profit continue in

the current path of doing both the CEO work and CFO work by the owner. While, the ones closer to the higher end, may decide to get a CFO earlier, they may decide to get a controller or hire a full-time accountant. This may be an alright decision for a short time, but it may be slowing the progress of the company and may take the necessary reporting tools away from the CEO. Hence, on the one hand, there may be a savings of $50 K - $100 K, in terms of costs, but the company may be losing multiples of this in terms of lost profits.

For these companies, it is wise to look at hiring a consultant to help out. Many good services are available, that act as a remote CFO which can help out for these exact needs. The services can be tailored to your exact requirements and size of your company. They can range in costs from $1 K to $ 5 K per month and is the perfect stepping stone before a company is financially ready to hire a full-time CFO. The great thing with this service is the company gets the use of a professional CFO with all the required education and expertise but does not have to hire them full-time. Hence, the costs are a fraction of what a full-time CFO would cost, but the benefits are still significant. The fact of the matter is that with smaller companies, a full-time CFO would not be required and would be too costly, but the small company can still benefit significantly from the help of a CFO. This would allow the CEO to focus on growing the business and provide comfort in knowing that the company and CEO is being assisted by a CFO with years of experience. This service can also grow with the business and up to the point where a full-time CFO would be of more benefit. The other advantage of this service is that it can be achieved remotely for the most part. There could be some in-house sessions required but much of the work can be done over the computer and through communication tools such as Skype. It is important that when you get this service, that you maintain the same CFO over a long period to maintain consistency and reduce any costs to get up to speed. It would not be ideal if the company keeps changing the CFO for you. This would lessen the expected results.

Remote CFO

Overall, this service can have a significant and positive impact on the company. While paying a fraction of the cost of a full-time CFO, the company will derive a significant portion of the benefits of having a CFO. In reality, a CFO does work eight hours a day or more, but much of that time is geared towards building his team and only a part of that time is preparing and reviewing financial analysis for the CEO. With this service, the CFO can dedicate his time to delivering the maximum value to the client. Will it be the same as having a full-time CFO? No, but if done properly the company should be able to benefit almost as much as having a full-time CFO while paying a fraction of the cost. To analyze this, let's say that a full-time CFO would be able to improve the company's bottom line by $100 K, but the overall cost of that CFO would be $200 K, this would be a net cost of $100 K. On the other hand, a remote CFO should be able to achieve similar results, so let us say that they can save $50 K - $75 K per year, but now their cost is only $35 K to $50 K, saving roughly $25 K per year after their costs. This is precisely why at this lower level of revenue and profit, a remote CFO makes better sense than a full-time CFO. While, if we are to compare this with a larger company, the numbers may change significantly. The CFO who may cost $200 K, may be able to save the company $500 K, hence, they will have a net effect of improving profitability by $300 K, while, if this is done by a remote CFO, they may be able to find a net improvement of $300 K, but with a cost of $100 K, while the net costs are much lower, the overall savings is only $200 K, compared to the $300 K with the full-time CFO. On top of this, there is the growth effect, the company would grow faster each year with the CFO and this would far outweigh these costs. In summary, for a larger company that is making profits in excess of $500 K, it would make sense to go with the full-time CFO.

In conclusion, the structure of the CFO is very much dependent on many factors, but one of the main factors would be the overall size and profitability of the company. In general, for those companies earning less than $ 50 K per year, the best concept is that the owner does the work of the CFO with some assistance from friends and colleagues or perhaps with the help of a bookkeeper. While for those companies with profits between $50 K and $ 500 K, the best solution would be to find a consultant or consulting firm that can offer services such as remote CFO. This would allow the company to derive much of the benefits and expertise of a CFO but without having to have the significant cost. Those companies making more than $500 K profits per year are most likely to benefit from hiring a full-time CFO. This will ensure that they are getting the full benefits and since they are a staff member, they are more likely to be able to retain this individual.

CHAPTER 22 - OVERALL CONCLUSIONS

The CFO plays an integral part of any company. This role ensures that the CEO and others within the company can make the best decisions possible. Where the CFO works best is where he partners well with the CEO. This will allow the CEO to benefit from the sound judgment of the CFO and this will allow the company to succeed.

The CFO must possess a keen understanding of business, sound management practices, finance, accounting, and leadership. The CFO must be a strong leader who is capable of influencing others both internally and externally. The key person that they must influence is the CEO. It would be impossible to have a successful CFO if they are not capable of influencing the CEO. You could have the most potentially successful CFO, but partner him with a CEO who is not that capable and decides not to adhere to the advice given by the CFO, then you might as well have the worst CFO because the best CFO will do nothing positive if the CEO is not paying attention to their advice. This situation can be resolved if the CFO does not report directly to the CEO, but instead reports to the Board.

Reporting Line

Our strong recommendation is that the CFO should not report directly to the CEO, but report directly to the Board, while the CEO can have an indirect reporting relationship and have oversight on the day to day activities of the CFO, they should be limited in many respects. This will allow the CFO to disagree with the CEO and allow for situations where a weak CEO who is in charge of a strong CFO is not permitted to exert undue pressure on the CFO, due to the reporting line structure. In this case, the weak CEO will be judged by the Board as well as the CFO for any disagreements. The CEO would not like to lose many of these battles, as such, they will be more likely to listen to a successful and strong CFO. This will benefit the CEO, by making better choices and benefit the company as well. It may seem that this relationship could be detrimental for both the CEO and CFO, but in reality, the opposite is true. They will be forced to come to a better understanding without the possibility of one simply ignoring the other.

Benefits of a CFO

It is clear that large companies benefit greatly from having a solid CFO, but very small ones may not be in a position to afford this. All companies big or small will benefit from a CFO, but for the small ones, the functions that they play are usually taken by the owner. When companies become large enough with net income more than $500 K, this is when they start to look for a full-time CFO. It may be wise to start earlier, but definitely by this level of profit, a full-time CFO should be considered. The CFO may well be able to benefit the company above their cost. Hence, if the company can grow at a rate of 10% with a CFO versus a rate of 5% without, then this small difference could have a significant effect on the bottom line. Let us say that the company has a profit of $500 K, but the overall revenues are $5 M, now let us say that the variable costs on revenues are 50%. Hence, if a company grows at 10%, they would now earn $500 K more but they would have increased expenses of $250 K, hence a net profit of $250 K. This may be compared to a net growth of $250 K with a net profit of $125 K. Hence, in the first year the CFO comes close to paying for their salary, but where the real value is that after seven years of this growth rate, the company now has doubled their revenue, hence it now has revenues of $10 M and their overall profitability, would now be approximate $5.5 M, while if there was no CFO hired and it grew at the rate of 5% per year, the growth would only be about 40%, hence the revenues would be about $7 M and now profits would be about $3.5 M. It is very clear that the added value of a strong CFO pays strong dividends down the road. As well, the sooner one hires a successful CFO, the sooner one starts to get stronger growth rates.

Generally, before a company hits about $500 K, it is very wise to hire a full-time CFO, unless, the owner of the company is a prior CFO, then they could play the role of both CFO and CEO, but very soon, they will run out of hours in the day and this would not be advisable for any real length of time. By having the CEO focus on CEO functions, this will also be of benefit to the company and the sooner there are two points of view on the way forward, the faster the company can grow.

Mid-Term Solutions

Before a company can achieve more than $500 K in profits per year, the company can hire a consultant who can take on the role of the part-time CFO. There are also services like Remote CFO that can help out for the smaller companies. This has the advantage of not having the high costs of hiring a full-time CFO but also provides the advantage of having the expertise of a CFO available to the company.

The added value of having the expert advice of a strong CFO can be the difference between a struggling company to one that is thriving and growing at a great rate. It is one thing to be consistently profitable over several years, but with strong growth of your company, your profits can grow at a much greater pace. In some cases, a small 5% increase in revenues can be the difference from losing money to making significant profits. Being able to determine the best prices, the best marketing strategy, and ensuring all departments have their reporting needs being met, can be the major difference to get the revenues to grow at a quicker rate.

Skill Sets

The CFO must have the proper skill sets and leadership abilities, but as well, they must have the proper prerequisites for success. If the business model of the company is not sound, the CFO cannot change it to make it that much better, they can sound the alarm that a change is required and perhaps a whole new segment needs to be chosen. This will be a key benefit, as knowing when there is something that can be fixed and knowing when something is beyond repair, is a great thing to know. Often, companies throw good money at bad money because it is hard to just accept a loss and move on. There are times when a company has invested a significant sum into a product that simply will never work, many will feel we already spent so much and what is a little more. The problem with this approach is that there is no end to it, a strong CFO will tell you that and it will be time to move on. There may be a loss, but the loss will be far less than if efforts were to be continued on a losing product or segment.

Ultimately the CFO is a critical component in the success of any company. Sometimes, they are at the forefront and sometimes in the background, but they are always a significant factor in the success of every company.

THANK YOU

Thank you for reading this book. We hope you enjoyed its content and would love to hear feedback from you. We also would love to be able to send you first drafts of our work, prior to publication for your feedback.

Scan for Feedback

To subscribe with us enter the following - **https://markgruner-.com/contact-us/subscribe/**

ABOUT THE AUTHOR

Mark Gruner

Mark Gruner is a professional financial accountant and adviser. He has worked throughout much of the World with international organizations. He has worked as Chief Financial Officer and most recently as Director of Finance. Mark studied at McGill University first doing an undergraduate degree in Science in Biochemistry. He later moved into the field of business and did his graduate degree in Public Accounting at McGill University in Montreal, Canada. After that he went on and wrote the Chartered Accounting exam and became a Chartered Accountant.

He has worked for large international organizations such as Internation Finance Corporation, part of the World Bank Group, and has worked in Asia, Africa, Europe, and North America.

BOOKS BY THIS AUTHOR

Money Matters For Personal Finance

No matter your financial situation - improve it!

This book will show you how to save on your costs, maximize your revenues and get the most out of your portfolios. We will show you how to invest your money to have a safe portfolio but yet very well-performing. These techniques beat out 90% of very well-paid Wall Street brokers.

The Principles Of Highly Successful Nonprofits

What makes a Nonprofit Successful?

There are key Principles to ensure success with nonprofits. This book is ideal for those that understand and work in nonprofits and also for those that intend to work with a nonprofit. Understanding these principles is paramount to achieving strong results. This book explains what good governance is and why it is crucial. These principles should be followed by all nonprofits but surprisingly only a handful of them do follow these principles. This is what divides the successful from the struggling nonprofit.

GET IN TOUCH WITH THE AUTHOR

Visit the author's site - **https://markgruner.com/**

For any feedback - **https://markgruner.com/contact-us/feed-back/**

For more direct help get in touch with Green Bridge Consulting - **https://greenbridgeco.com/** or scan QR code

ACKNOWLEDGEMENT

Thanks for support from my readers and my business partner Joshua Brugger.

I would also like to thank my past staff members who have always been a huge support to my work and have worked with me to get my visions to come true.

www.ingramcontent.com/pod-product-compliance
Lightning Source LLC
Chambersburg PA
CBHW051833130726
47987CB00002B/530